RED CARPET DIARIES

RED CARPET DIARIES

Confessions of
A Glamour Boy

STEVEN COJOCARU

BALLANTINE BOOKS • NEW YORK

A Ballantine Book
Published by The Ballantine Publishing Group

Copyright © 2003 by Steven Cojocaru

www.ballantinebooks.com

Book design by Joseph Rutt

Library of Congress Cataloging-in-Publication Data
Cojocaru, Steven.
    Red carpet diaries / Steven Cojocaru.—1st ed.
      p. cm.
    ISBN 0-345-45378-6
    1. Cojocaru, Steven.   2. Journalists—Canada—Biography.   I. Title.
PN4913.C59A3 2003
070.92—dc21
    [B]

                                                            2002043650

Manufactured in the United States of America

First Edition: March 2003

10 9 8 7 6 5 4 3

This book is dedicated to that barely five-foot-tall spitfire, my mom, Amelia. If angels in disguise do inhabit this earth, they have honey-hued highlights and a collection of Gucci-logo bags (painstakingly wrapped in tissue paper, of course).

For better or worse (I'm talking about my 1980s heavy-metal hair here), this saga is absolutely true. Still, in order to save myself from getting socked over the head with an imitation Vuitton tote bag or being banished from Passover dinners, some of the names of relatives, family acquaintances, and high school peers have been changed to protect the not-well-accessorized.

CONTENTS

ACKNOWLEDGMENTS

I'd probably be employed as Jennifer Lopez's laundress and rinsing out her glow-in-the-dark panties right now if not for the extraordinarily lovely human beings who believed in this wayward waif with a dream . . .

Benjamin Cojocaru—the most devoted dad an untamable son could ever ask for. I know I gave you every single gray strand on your head—the offer to send you a year's supply of Just For Men (in sandy blond shade) still stands.

Alisa Cojocaru—the most teased sister in history. I still owe you moola from when you scraped every penny you had together to help bankroll my journey to Hollywood. Can I pay you in shoes?

Shari Isenberg, Abby Finer, and Shane Brolly—The best-friend committee/my other family. I'd probably be on a Prozac IV drip if I didn't have you to lean on. "Thank you" doesn't even begin to cover it. Thank you for propping me up, paying

my phone bills when I was a starving scribe, and being there—
no matter what.

Carol Wallace—you took me from nothing and made
something out of me. I'll always be grateful to you.

Rob "My Secret Weapon" Silverstein. Thank you for saying
I could when everyone else said I couldn't.

Katie, Matt, Ann, and Al—you have been far more generous and hospitable to me than you ever had to be. Thank you,
America's classiest first TV family, for even giving this nutjob
the time of day.

Ken "The Architect" Slotnick, Nora "The Savior" McAniff,
Martha Nelson, Bonnie "The Mentor" Johnson, Heidi "The
Other Sister" Markel, Jay Mandel, Allison Dickens, Sarajane
"Director of Everything" Sparks, Jeanne Newman, Monica
"Puppet" Rizzo, Susan Ollinick, Dan Osheyack, Marcy "My
Obsession" Engelman, Todd Gold, Elycia "The New Jackie O"
Rubin, Betsy Alexander (I'm glad I listened to you and ditched
the Fu Manchu beard), Jessica Cesa (behind the silly TV clown
is the talented producer), Tobie Rozakalis Loomis, Stinky B.
Cojocaru, Jennifer "I'd Be Naked if Not for You" Wallace, Amy
Koch, John Griffiths, Samanatha McIntyre, Steve and Linda
Levine, Rick Glassman, Kimberly Hovey, Cindy Murray,
Heather Smith, and the director of my hair and best girlfriend
ever . . .

Byron Williams.

And to the so-called misfits out there struggling to find their
way in a harsh world. There is hope . . .

NOT JUST ANOTHER VERSACE OPENING

Beverly Hills, December 1997

L et me make something perfectly clear: I am not an ashtray. Though it's quite a stretch to confuse a person with an object used to stub out burning matter, **Donatella Versace** somehow managed to make this creative leap. I did nothing to encourage her—except for wearing a smashing (if highly flammable) knee-length white mink coat with a 1970s-vintage pedigree. A rock-star-worthy cloak worn for cheap attention? Guilty. But I was competing with the decor of the most salaciously decked-out faux palazzo this side of Portofino and the hot pink snakeskin toilet seat covers were winning.

I love cobblestone streets as much as the next romantic, but not when I'm staggering around on four-inch-heeled platform boots that once belonged to one of the members of Ratt. Still, that's a footwear hazard you risk when you're making your way to Versace's new shopping shrine on Via Rodeo, a European-flavored annex to Rodeo Drive dotted with Old World street lamps and New World retail playgrounds like Tiffany & Co. and Charles Jourdan.

Everything is marble. What hasn't been poured and cemented (which would include the bevy of Beverly Hills socialites on hand) appears to have been dipped in gold. It's a heady design scheme that screams "Queen of Babylon's mausoleum meets the baccarat room at Bellagio." Anchoring it all is the penile equivalent of steps, a powerfully sweeping staircase I suspect single-handedly depleted the world's supply of flecked limestone. I guzzle a couple of vodka tonics and suddenly I'm picturing a high-on-Ecstasy Scarlett O'Hara in a zebra-patterned catsuit and patent leather stilettos. "Welcome to Club Tara," she booms to the crowd. "As G-d is my witness, I'll never miss a rave again!"

I take the stairway to sequined-sheath heaven and at the top, under the gigantic domed ceiling, She stands. Donatella. The mistress of the house is even more fabulously, aggressively Donatellian than I imagined. The Lady Godiva mane so platinum-borderline-institutional-white I wonder if some Milanese colorist named Fabrizzio invented a secret hair-tinting technique involving Liquid Paper. Not one inch of her epidermis is untanned. It's a deep charring I'm certain is only achieved by sleeping in a rotisserie oven.

Showtime: I'm feeling pretty dandy in my fuzzy coat thrown on top of my slight shoulders, leaving an intentionally clear view of my clingy black top that brazenly says "Fuck Me I'm Famous" in rhinestones. Now would be a good time to head out onto the balcony of this temple where Donatella and the other nicotine junkies are squeezed together. She's standing beside me sucking on a cigarette and speaking with her hands to minions. I don't interrupt, preferring to have a smoke and maybe do a little eavesdropping. As I'm puffing away grandly and starting to get lost in my head, some guy starts hitting me and screeching in a foreign tongue. My immediate thought is "I'm being pounded on by an envious party maggot because I look so fetching tonight." I'm wrong. "Your coat is on fire!" the accented pretty boy is screaming as he swats my sleeve until the flame is out. I look down and he's right. Her Blondness has been accidentally flecking her burning cinders onto my coat. But it can't possibly be. My plush cover-up is on loan from the top vintage boutique in Los Angeles.

I don't know what pisses me off more: finding myself swathed in a scorched time-share mink or noting that my assailant stands by during the bonfire and barely blinks? A little love would be welcome—hold me, Donatella—and not a look in her bored eyes that says, "Big deal. I light people on fire at all my parties."

Welcome to my world.

ONE

THE GREEN CHIFFON MASTERPIECE

You don't argue with the dress code to the event of the year. My mom wouldn't dare. In her world, a bedroom community in the English-speaking part of Montreal, nothing less than a sartorial grand slam was expected for the social earthquake that would maritally merge Shirley "the brassiere tycoon's daughter" Glick with Stanley "balding but heir to a fortune made in freeze-dried noodles" Fleischman. When the Princess telephone in my mom's violet boudoir started ringing off the hook with friends calling to participate in the "what are you wearing to the wedding?" squawk-a-thon, I knew this wasn't going to be pretty. Not with a pack of gold-lamé-addicted vulturettes pitted against each other in the Most To-Die-For Dress showdown.

Romanian émigrée ladies, start your engines.

My mom had an edge over all the Zsa Zsa wannabes flocking to the Elizabeth Hager boutique in the Cavendish Mall for a

Bob Mackie knockoff. She could whip up her own creation. Not to brag, but I was the son of the only seamstress for miles who was famed for her magic hands. Still, to call Amelia Cojocaru a seamstress wasn't quite right. She was an artiste, a master, the Coco Chanel of Melling Avenue. Or at least in my dazzled orbs she was. And that wasn't a used Singer sewing machine unit blemished with cracked wood crammed into a corner of our kitchen. This was a grand atelier in Paris and contessas swathed in ermine were sweeping in for couture fittings. And out of this renowned fashion house came a gown of such dizzying, stupefying glamour it can only be dubbed The Green Chiffon Masterpiece.

I saw it assembled bit by luscious bit. A dark-green-beaded bodice for that gleaming-emeralds effect. Just below, a smart velvet sash. The flowing floor-length skirt that made an almost melodic soft whooshing sound when Mom picked it up. It was a zippered dream that could provoke even a chaste woman to lose herself and wantonly drink kosher wine from her silver leather pump.

After months of my barreling in from kindergarten and watching this exquisite puzzle being put together, Project X was ready for unveiling and I was about to perform my first fashion critique. Against the backdrop of an homage-to-Versailles bedroom laden with fake-gold-accented furniture, a porcelain-skinned, raven-haired vision in a cloud of chiffon twirled. My review, perhaps not as zingy or polished as what I'd eventually become known for, was an instant breathless rave: "Mom, you look like Elizabeth Taylor!"

Not bad for mom—a saucy import from Bucharest. But as my mother points out, Bucharest was the Paris of Romania in her day. During her childhood, sweet-faced blue-eyed girls like her were reared with piano lessons, perfect manners, and proper wardrobes long on fussy ribbons, lace knickers, and bonnets.

Her own Richard Burton, Benjamin Cojocaru, grew up on the wrong side of the Transylvania peaks, in a no-name village in the Romanian countryside. Their paths didn't cross until they fled postwar Romania and met in Israel, where they both landed in the 1950s. Every Friday night Amelia would take a break from studying fashion design and make a pilgrimage to the cinema, where she'd float away in an Elizabeth Taylor or Lana Turner haze. Ben was a sharp dresser given to sporting silk cravats who met Amelia at a luncheon tossed by mutual friends. They flirted over a Middle Eastern feast featuring an all-the-hummus-you-can-eat spread. By the time the dip was gone, Ben was delirious over the bombshell from Bucharest. He walked Amelia home and asked her to go to the cinema that night. He chose well—*A Place in the Sun* starring Elizabeth Taylor. Ben might have been from the wrong side of the tracks, but Amelia was beginning to thaw.

Ben had some competition: Amelia was already dating Larry, a blue-eyed golden boy who was the **Brad Pitt** of Haifa. Except, Larry had one problem: He was a rat exterminator. No matter how much cologne Larry poured all over himself, he couldn't shake the scent of rat poison. So it was bye-bye to Eau de Rat, and hello to Ben's poison-free musk. (During my childhood, when my parents would "have words," my mother would hiss, "I should have married Larry." My father would shoot back with, "Oh yeah, the rat exterminator." Then my mother would suck me into the fracas. "If I married Larry, honey, you would have big blue eyes," she would say. And I'd go, "But then the house would reek of rat poison.")

My parents loved their life in Israel, but they moved to Canada to make a good life for their future family. My dad had an aunt in Montreal who sponsored them. Auntie was an old-school Romanian woman built like a brick outhouse. She frightened me. She flung around the most humongous breasts I'd ever seen. Every time she hugged me I was terrified I would fall into the abyss of her cleavage never to be seen again. To this day I have a big-heaving-bosom fear. It's a clinical disorder marked by feelings of unbearable suffocation. Looking at **Pamela Anderson** seems to trigger the most virulent attacks.

I was "different" from the get-go. I felt like I had been born into the wrong place, the wrong body, the wrong hair. When my parents used to argue with me, I threatened to call Monte Carlo because I was convinced that I was Princess Grace and Prince Rainier's love-child. My only consolation was my mother's rabid fashion sense. She dressed me like a ventriloquist's dummy, in miniature velvet blazers and matching shorts, and I loved it (except for the ties). She decided the only garb worthy of her pride and joy had to come from the Little Lord Fauntleroy catalog: pressed shirts with polka dots, silk hankies nattily peeking out from their front pockets, and the like. She would have pressed my Adidas sneakers if she'd had the technology. But the fussing was worth it. Clothing was a language in my family, and my mother was fluent. On perfect summer days, she and I used to walk together down bustling St. Catherine Street in Montreal, her in an off-white tunic-and-pants ensemble and me in a nautical navy blazer with white pants. We were a Xerox copy of Jackie O and JFK Jr. and I thought we were beautiful.

THE CRAZY UNCLE THEORY

I think the Crazy Uncle theory can be applied here. I've always held that every family has a delightfully zany uncle, and I have an inkling I'm the nutcase future relatives will buzz about. I can see an oil painting of me hanging over the fireplace in the family manor and I'll be draped in a fluorescent blue Cavalli leather jumpsuit. My grandnephews will say, "Oh, that's our wacko Uncle Steven. He passed away at 104 freebasing Botox on a yacht in Sardinia. It was a sad ending. Very hush-hush."

Even as a kid, I was obsessed with style. I had long, wild hair and I wanted a groovy shag like Rod Stewart. But when I was about ten, my mother could no longer deal with it. She couldn't comprehend my mangy locks—they weren't "proper."

I think this must be Grade 1 or 2. I hated ties then, and I hate them now. This is a Well-Behaved-Little-Prince look my Mom put together. The hanky is a nice touch, though, Mom. *(Photo courtesy of the author)*

So after a protracted negotiation—eureka, I was allowed to stay up for *Charlie's Angels*—we agreed that I would subject myself to a "little trim."

I wanted to go where my glamour-puss mom went—where you made appointments in advance, where there were *Vogue* magazines and coffee. Instead, she took me to a shanty house for my hair. A barbershop with, God forbid, a barber pole. No valet parking. No frappuccino. Then she sat me down in the chair and yammered to the barber in Romanian. I had no idea what they were saying until he started hacking my hair off. Ambush! My hair was in the middle of a fashion assassination.

Halfway through, with my heart in my throat, I vaulted out of my seat and tore out of the fluorescent-lit dump. I raced through the streets until I found a safe house, the shopping mall. I said to myself, "I will teach my mom a lesson. I'm going to let her think I was abducted." So I stayed in the mall for hours. I returned home that night just in time to stop the picture of me in a powder-blue snowsuit from being printed on milk cartons.

No one would have recognized me anyway. I was now modeling an edgy, half-short half-long do that Vidal Sassoon would have drooled over. Mom elected to face the problem by using the predictable reverse psychology tactic. "Fine, walk around looking like that. I don't care," she said through tight lips. I heard her choke out that sentence a lot over the next week. I finally caved when my dad presented a most attractive offer to me—an extra five bucks added to my birthday score if I ditched my striking avant-garde hairstyle. I learned an important life lesson: Money talks, and I could be bought. And a second lesson: Hair is everything.

It was all Romania's fault. Not just the barbershop incident and the shearing orders given in what I perceived was a primitive, gypsy tongue. As far as I was concerned, Romania was to blame for everything. If my parents hadn't been from Lower Moldavia, I wouldn't have had such a hard time adjusting to my universe. I wouldn't have had to explain their unnatural obsession with gymnast Nadia Comaneci to my friends. Or hide their collection of Bucharestian Big Band records. And I would never ever have to look at a plate of that Romanian delicacy, boiled cabbage à l'Orange. Mom sensed how desperate I was to assimilate. She spoke only English to me, even if she did sound like Vlad the Impaler. She had then and continues to have the thickest—though utterly charming—accent. She still sounds like the receptionist at the Transylvania Comfort Inn.

They should have just operated the Romanian embassy out of our home. Our neighbors had living rooms, but we entertained out of a much more Continental space dubbed The Salon. Not that I was invited on the official tour. Mom worried that I'd splatter chocolate milk all over her perfect Romanian French provincial lair—it was a rather irrational fear considering that the hermetically sealed-in-plastic furnishings could have survived a nuclear blast. But why risk damaging a gold-embroidered white damask chaise that was Louis the Fourteenth meets Louis Moscovitch Discount Furniture? Alas, things have not changed. My happily retired parents, now installed in a nice all-white apartment in a nice doorman building, still impose martial law on their property. When I visit, Mom gently suggests that I might want to shower in the health club down the street so "the wallpaper in the guest bathroom won't peel."

My far-less-rambunctious-than-me sister was exempt from the restricted airspace over The Salon regulation. But she never ventured out from her bedroom anyway. She was permanently

It was all Romania's fault. Not just the barbershop incident and the shearing orders given in a primitive gypsy tongue. As far as I was concerned, Romania was to blame for everything. If my parents hadn't been from Lower Moldavia, I wouldn't have had such a hard time adjusting to my universe.

parked in front of her makeup mirror trying to re-create Cheryl Tiegs's makeup on herself. No one has seen Alisa without mascara and smoky magenta eye shadow since she graduated from her training bra. She's the looker of us two. The Jewish Heather Locklear in micro minis and stilettos (even when she's jogging).

We were forced to get along. Alisa and I shared a room, but I was apparently just an afterthought, much like an old floor lamp you stick in the bedroom because you have no other place for it. At least that's how I took it. How could I feel welcome in a little girl's room decorated with pink furniture? Was it any wonder I tossed and turned all night when sleeping on a bed that had a pink headboard with a giant poodle stencil drawing on it?

The Jewish Heather Locklear
(Photo courtesy of the author)

Once I started kindergarten, I got upgraded to my very own bedroom. It was all blue and nobody bothered to get my input on the color scheme. When somebody asked me my favorite color, my mother would interrupt, *"Blue!* He loves blue!" She fitted my room with a coarse two-toned blue shag rug. The bed had a fancy spread that was a duvet with blue plaid. The walls were painted a royal blue with a blue gloss finish. Except the bed set was still my sister's old, pink one. My father hand-painted it

Cousin Maryann *(left)*, me, and my sister, Alisa. My ventriloquist's dummy look is courtesy of my mom. *(Photo courtesy of the author)*

brown and then swiped it with this special teak glaze. But I knew what it really looked like. That bed set was such a profound symbol for who I was: Everything appeared blah brown on the outside, but on the inside, I was more of a blazing fuchsia.

Television saved me from my brown-but-wish-it-was-fuchsia world. It brought a gorgeous pointy-headed alien into my life. She was beamed into my bedroom. I wasn't scared. Actually, I got a warm feeling all over my eight-year-old body. Sure she had arms and legs and could speak. But she couldn't be real or something as mundane as a human. On careful inspection, there was something eerily familiar about this fantastic apparition in sequins. Below the feather headdress was a long face with sharp angles like mine. Were we from the same DNA? Why did our cheekbones, our colorings match? Where were the rest of our people? I asked my mom when this startling life-force living inside my television would be back again. "Oh, darling, that's **Cher,**" she bubbled. "She's on every week."

Cher was my very own visual tsunami. Watching the *The*

Sonny and Cher Comedy Hour was like having my birthday, Hanukkah, and losing my virginity every week. Cher understood. She brought me back to the mother ship. Quickly, she was joined by **Mick Jagger** in the V.I.P. room of my psyche. He was an androgynous dandy with eyeliner and wrapped in a multitude of silk scarves in screaming bright colors. I thought he had fallen from the sky. Up until I saw him, I believed I was the only male on earth saddled with lips that could swallow a multilevel parking structure. Finally, I had found my tribe—I loved the way these two looked, the way they moved. I wasn't alone any longer. "That's it," I thought. "These two are my real parents. I must join them in their land."

> ## WHAT I LEARNED ABOUT FASHION FROM MY MOM
>
> • Gold lamé is the new black.
>
> • Big hair has a religious purpose. "Tease your hair really high—you'll be closer to the Almighty"—Amelia Cojocaru, 1978.
>
> • Caftans were invented so women could eat all the cheesecake they want.

But first, I had to get through the minefield that was my childhood.

TWO

——m——

THE FREAK
SHOW IN NOIR

Can a style-hungry eleven-year-old be blamed for crashing his sister's fashion party? Alisa was in high school now and she and her groovy friends were having a major fashion moment. When they weren't at Chez Cojocaru ironing their hair, they were camped out at hipster store Le Chateau. This is where cool kids snapped up the most unlikely of must-have accessories: wooden clogs with glossy leather finishings.

Go ahead and think unibrowed granola-ite plodding around in her unseemly clunky clogs if you must. But these show-off shoes were the Manolo Blahniks of their day. Their upscale Boho look coordinated perfectly with the wild super-sized bell-bottoms dubbed "elephant pants" that any self-respecting sixteen-year-old chick taking style cues from **Marcia Brady** and **Farrah Fawcett** possessed. Elephant pants were skintight at the bum and crotch and then each leg exploded into yards of wide fabric, not all that far from looking like te-pees in transit.

I was determined to steal this look no matter what it took. Even if that meant begging my dad for a cash advance on my college tuition along with the humiliation of sauntering into Le Chateau and getting treated like a kindergartner who somehow slipped off his leash. Got the clogs—check. Hello, Howick Big Star elephant pants. Top it all off with a clingy polyester "disco" shirt. It was

No, it's not the Osbournes, but something almost as scary: The 1970s Nuclear Family portrait! *(Photo courtesy of the author)*

John Travolta artfully fused with Marcia and Farrah. I was primed to make my debut.

I don't know why I didn't feel any fear about a Grade Fiver sweeping into the schoolyard in anything but the official uniform of Levis and Keds. I guess it was the charge of making my first grand entrance that propelled me forward as I swaggered to school (as much as one can swagger in elephant pants), adrenaline pumping all the way. As I made my final approach, I was exhilarated. I looked so superstylish, certain that I was the be-all and end-all of grade school chic. And then the bomb fell. Just as I swept in and waved at my friends playing dodgeball, a schoolmate named Peter snarled at me, "Steven, what are you wearing? You look like a girl!"

Somebody else chimed in, "Yeah, you look like a girl." And

One year's disaster can be next year's catwalk sensation.

then a third person said, "A girl. Yep. Totally." In my head, it felt like a stadium of a hundred thousand snickering kids. I had tears in my eyes. My big fashion statement was imploding and it continued to implode. All throughout the day, I heard these sneers: "Steven is a girl. You look like a girl." My face was flaming red. I just wanted to walk right out of the clothes, out of my life.

But this is a lesson you learn:

One year's disaster can be next year's catwalk sensation.

Greg Brady, eat your heart out! This is me in grade 3 or 4. I lived for this shirt. I thought it was so spiffy and groovy. It's the first piece of clothing I really felt stylish in. *(Photo courtesy of the author)*

Fast forward to 2000. I'm still aping Greg Brady in vintage Pucci spiffy and groovy shirts. *(Photo courtesy of People magazine)*

I wore my outfit again a year later and it worked better. I put it in mothballs and treated it like a Vera Wang wedding gown. Three years later, surprise, surprise, all the kids were wearing my outfit, not as fetchingly as I had, I might say. At that point, I had already moved on to white leather.

Every little Jewish Romanian prince has a big red carpet moment.

In the Jewish religion, your bar mitzvah is a religious ceremony followed by a party to signify leaving boyhood at age thirteen and becoming a man (even if your legs are as smooth and hairless as **Sarah Michelle Gellar**'s in a slit evening gown). You go to Hebrew school and learn the prayers. But I must confess: I'm a Hebrew school dropout. My expulsion occurred when I gave my teacher's bright orange beehive the once-over and proceeded to call her Mrs. Tangerine Head (which I repeated about five hundred times until she claimed a blood vessel in her head was about to blow). So she had me kicked out, leaving me ill-prepared to perform my Bar Mitzvah prayers. Canceling my bar mitzvah was out of the question—what would the relatives say?—so my parents were forced to enroll me in a Bar Mitzvah for Dummies accelerated class. Instead of studying the chants for a year like I was supposed to, an "arrangement" was made to have me privately tutored by a rent-a-rabbi with a wart on his nose the size of Tel Aviv.

The Cojocaru clan's bar mitzvah party ensembles fell under the strict dictate of my mom. She had a concept (actually, a

mystical vision) that my dad and I were going to wear matching tuxedos, and she and Alisa were going to be swathed in
matching frocks. For her "men," she selected powder-blue tuxedos with ruffled shirts and navy velvet bow ties—very Wayne-
Newton posse. Mom and Alisa were to make the scene in
look-alike mint-green dresses. Too bad the powder blue and
the mint green had no connection whatsoever. In the family
photos, we look like discarded M&Ms.

The day of my bar mitzvah, something profound and
deeply spiritual happened to me: I had my first professional
blowout. Mom took me to a fancy men's hair salon called Le
Pascha, which was rife with rich geezers getting their comb-
overs coifed and mega sprayed to the point of shellacking. The
adrenaline rush for me was almost too much to bear: the round
brush touching my scalp, the blast of hot air tickling my neck.
When I looked up, I had long hair. For a shiny-tamed-tresses
moment I looked the way I wanted to. I was Mick Jr. (with
maybe an unintentional hint of Valerie Bertinelli)—milky-white
skin, big juicy lips, and hair curtaining straight down my face
for the first time.

If a bomb had hit upscale Chinese eatery Ruby Foo's on
the night of my bar mitzvah, there would have been nary a
fifty-something Romanian woman with tufts of chin hair left
in Montreal. Everywhere I looked these gorillas draped in chiffon were shoveling miniature egg rolls into their mouths. I
warned my friends not to wave their fingers lest they be mis-
taken for pot stickers. Then a horrible gypsy creature
swooped in. Marianna was a belly dancer my parents had

hired to entertain the crowd. She had a jet-black mane that fell all the way to her behind, spoonfuls of neon blue eye shadow, and a waist thickened by too much rich Romanian grub. I took an instant dislike to this low-rent, bloated version of Cher. How dare she steal my thunder? Worse, she had the nerve to violate my personal space and jiggle her breasts in the bar mitzvah boy's face. She kept stiffly smiling to the crowd after I whispered in her ear that I was going to attack her with a wok.

The night was big for me, because I decided to have my first real decadent moment: guzzling a whiskey sour. Actually, since the bartender was so busy salivating over Marianna, he neglected to card anybody, and I downed about a dozen drinks. I started getting dizzy during the final chorus of "Hava Nagila" and right there on the dance floor vomited all over my rented power-blue tux. Then I threw up in the car on the way home. I felt awful and delirious but I had my first taste of the rock-star life and it had me in its thrall.

Until my bar mitzvah, I had a lot of friends. But then in one fell swoop, they vanished. The first sign of trouble was sports. The huge question in Canada was, "Why doesn't he like hockey?" I think there was a town council meeting about why I didn't like hockey. It's ironic because I do like hockey. My dad used to take me to hockey games and I liked going, and not just for the uniforms. I liked watching it. I've always liked being a specta-tor. It's like going to a fashion show except the models have chipped teeth. But exerting myself and chasing a puck was certainly not on my agenda.

It was a painful transition from popularity to pariah. This situation was not helped by my disastrous looks, a prequel to the Goth fad duds. I just gave up on my bushy hair and let it grow to the proportions of a tumbleweed. Before braces and much later becoming a teeth-bleaching junkie, I had so many huge yellow overlapping teeth I thought I was part horse. If the top of me was writ large, from the neck down I was puny Olive Oyl with arms and legs the width of dental floss. *Homely* didn't even begin to cover it.

So I went into my black period. I shrouded myself in black gear all the time. I signed a long-term lease for the bunker when I entered high school. The only safe place was my all-blue bedroom. Door shut, baby-blue silk curtains drawn, complete blackout save for the flickering images from my proudest possession, my very own twenty-six-inch hand-me-down Sanyo TV. The only company I had in the bunker were the airbrushed mugs of **Cheryl Ladd** and **Bo Derek** gazing at me from the posters that covered the walls.

My reading materials consisted solely of *People* magazines. I was quickly earning my Ph.D. in celebrity. Like a Socrates of the suburbs, my mind wrestled with the substantive questions of the day. "So where is this place called Studio 54 and do people really shed their clothes and boogie all night in a drug-induced trance?" An even greater philosophical conundrum plagued me: "Do Jerry Hall and Bianca Jagger detest each other?"

My extensive knowledge of all things glam didn't endear me to my peers. Nothing was more torturous—not even the recurring nightmare I had of Marianna forcing me to belly dance with her at gunpoint—than being excluded from hanging around the "popular" entrance at recess and lunch at my high school. Sure, I could have just walked over, but I thought I'd be stoned to death. Instead, I was relegated to the "freak" entrance just around the corner. We would all hang out on the stairs— the stoners, the bad elements, the punk girls, and the lonely weirdos like me.

I escaped the blue bunker by my midteens and decided I had no choice but to accept full freakdomship. What the freaks did best was cut school and hang at the mall. The Cavendish Mall had become the epicenter of social life in my neighborhood, and my school was about eight blocks away. You could not keep me away from it.

The fact was, the Elizabeth Hager women's boutique was there—a soothing, womblike place I had visited countless times with my mom. The clothes brought such a reaction in me: I would get the high-fashion willies. When my mom said she was going to Elizabeth Hager, I always answered, "Oh, you could maybe drag me there. I'll go kicking and screaming." But I was really bursting to go. I used to scan the racks and give my mom advice. At fourteen years old, I would tell her, "No, no, no, no, no. I see you more in a sheath dress." Or, "Mom, I think you need more slacks and maybe more of a stacked heel." She'd listen to me completely. So cutting school at the mall was kind of bittersweet for me, because I couldn't go in Elizabeth

Hager alone or with my friends. I was scared they would have put a transsexual label on my head. But I wanted to be close to it. I wanted to know it was nearby.

The misfit mafia got old, though. Pappa needed a brand-new bag (or at least a less morose group of friends). Then something happened that every in-genue hopes for: I was discovered! By the most popular girl in our hemisphere, no less. Shari Isen-berg was the de facto queen of our high school. She had the looks—a Jaclyn Smith dead ringer with dark feathered hair, hazel-green eyes, porcelain skin, and bee-stung cherry-hued lips. She was in the minute per-centile of girls in our school whose tiny delicate nose hadn't been renovated by nose-job king Dr. Caplan and his construction crew. She cer-

Shari Isenberg—the most popular girl in high school (Shari Isenberg)

tainly had the social credentials along with the right wardrobe—Daddy was a real estate magnate and his princess had a different cashmere sweater (sorbet colors only) for all eight days of Hanukkah and more to spare.

Shari was also pure turbo-charged evil. And she saved her most sadistic behavior for wrong-side-of-the-tracks Mona, whose mother worked as the housekeeper for Shari's family.

Mona got Shari's Ralph Lauren hand-me-downs along with a lot of grief. "That's my sweater," Shari would hiss at Mona in class. The abuse was unrelenting until the day I saw Shari running to the principal's office with blood dripping down to the oversized collar of her raccoon coat. I had to stand outside and listen. Shari screamed in her Queen Bitch voice that Mona had up and socked her in the mouth. Deep breathing exercises saved me from cheering at the top of my lungs.

No one was sure if it was Mona's powerful left hook or a couple of productive sessions with an exorcist, but Shari was soon morphing into a reasonable facsimile of a human being. A month after the Mona incident, she tried to chat me up in English class. My first reflex was to hold up a cross and spit chewed-up garlic cloves at her. Little did I know then that she had already selected me as her pet sociological project. Shari was nobly attempting to be a more charitable person, and she figured there was no better place to start than with the freak show in *noir*. I couldn't have done better to improve my social standing if I had hired Joan Collins's publicist.

It didn't take long for me to bring out Shari's quirky side and for her to anoint me her official fashion consultant. My muse stoked the fashion fire within me. Soon sartorial declarations tripped off my tongue: "More feathered flips, Shari. Big hair is now," I proclaimed. And with her Good Jewish Housekeeping stamp of approval, I started advising all the popular girls.

I couldn't have done better to improve my social standing if I had hired Joan Collins's publicist.

They were captivated by my fashion ideas—and I had endless fashion ideas. Like shoes. Sometimes you have to go the distance for footwear. I thought cowboy boots were the next big thing. But you couldn't get them in Montreal. I made my parents drive me to Plattsburgh, New York, so I could spend an entire day going from store to store for the perfect western boots. I started hyperventilating when my eyes fixed on a chocolate-colored, intricately stitched pair. I lived in them, and soon enough everybody wanted a pair. Then came the construction-worker phase. You needed to wear striped Levis overalls—and you only fastened one side of them—a T-shirt, and construction boots with the laces undone. We had to go to a uniform store to get them. Mom, is this where the Village People shop?

It can be such a burden being the Halston of high school. After declaring that thin was in to my stable, I took a hard look at myself and saw how junk-food binges had taken a toll on my abs. We were all put on a rice cake diet immediately. Since I was in charge of so *It can be such a burden being the Halston of high school.* many waistlines, I felt the pressure to have all the answers and deliver quick results. When I saw an ad for a new diet pill called Dexatrim, my devious mind got to work. They weren't sold in Canada, so I picked some up the next time the family went on a Plattsburgh outing. Funny thing about diet pills that were later rumored to contain speed—the girls couldn't get enough of them. Within weeks, it seemed that everybody was coming to me for "Dexies." Yesterday's outcast was now running a drug cartel that could have rivaled Pablo Escobar's.

I thought volunteer stylists with a contraband diet pill side-line don't get to go to the ball. But you never know when a Rory Small is going to enter the picture. Rory was a fully-striped "popular girl." The daughter of one of the most loaded clans in our community. She was also what was gently referred to as "a big-boned girl." When she approached me at the cool entrance and started talking about the prom, my first thought was, "I hope they have a Plus Size prom dress rack at Elizabeth Hager." But Rory wasn't hitting me up for fashion advice. She was—whoa—asking *me* to be her date. I left my body at that point. My soaring spirit was already hitchhiking its way to Le Chateau for a natty ensemble.

I tried ignore my parents' rants about my severe weight loss. I was so pumped up on Dexies at this point—eleven days to the prom and I will be a Mick Jaggeresque stick figure—that it wasn't hard to block them out. Besides the constant shaking, my hearing was being muffled by regular ringing noises. Me and the folks were at Le Chateau, and I was mod-eling my prom look for their approval. So what if the ecru-colored blazer was a puny size 36 Long and still had to be taken in? It barely registered when the salesclerk sniffed that he had no dress shirts my size and that I might want to try the Evening Wear for Prepubescents section at a department store. I was too distracted by the most beautiful pair of shoes I'd ever seen: tan lace-ups with a fabulous light glaze on them that almost made them glow in the dark. The only pair they had left were two sizes too big. Perfect, I thought, the shoes are so noticeably gigantic, they'll draw attention away from the fact that Mr. Toothpick is being swallowed by his garb.

Alas, the skateboards disguised as footwear didn't fool Rory's parents. I arrived—via the white limo my parents popped for—at the Smalls' sprawling split-level digs with a gardenia corsage and a full heart. At the door was Rory shrouded in a baggy blue silk pantsuit. Behind her stood a professional photographer her parents hired to capture the golden prom couple. But why the tight smiles on the Smalls' faces? And why the huddle with the shutterbug?

I didn't understand why a plant was strategically placed in front of Rory as the shot was set up. Or why we posed behind a love seat. I was dumbfounded weeks later when I asked Rory about the pictures and she looked down at the ground and murmured that the film had been spoiled. How could ten rolls be spoiled? Then it hit me: Next to skeletal me, Rory must have appeared to be the size of the food court at the Cavendish Mall.

Then an even harsher reality finally sank in: At last I saw how I had wasted away to practically nothing. It was time to kick my habit cold turkey, retire from the Dexie trade and graduate from high school. I may have been emaciated, but I was determined to move forward and (ha!) lead the life of an intellectual (a leather-clad intellectual, of course).

THREE

BEWARE THE OVERSEXED SWEDE WITH NATURALLY HUMONGOUS BREASTS

I nga wanted off the private plane bad. It was a mistake to wing to Monte Carlo with a beast like Carlo Beradini. All those millions and he still had bad breath and a pot belly. She also regretted wearing a Saint Laurent ultrasuede mini with no undies.

Carlo put his grubby fingers on her thigh and starting panting. Inga said she wasn't feeling well but Carlo said he would make her feel better. "No means no Carlo," she answered.

But he held her down while shoving his hand up her skirt and moaning. Inga had an idea. "Ooh, bad bad Carlo," she squealed. "You like games too?" That got Carlo grunting and naked within seconds. Inga smiled at the beast and fished for her Hermés silk scarves. "Let's go wild in the shower. Wet and flying above the Riviera," she purred. She tied him to the showerhead and said she was going to get something to drink. She slammed the door shut and took her seat. When the hunky Greek copilot came out of the cockpit to investigate the screams he was hearing, Inga let him bang her. She owed it to him for saving her from Carlo.

• • •

If not for German Expressionist cinema, I might never have written my smash trashy novel, *The Exploits of Inga*. The above prose is just a snippet. You would have had to have been a habitué of the cafeteria at Dawson College to get your hands on the full body of work. I didn't set out to pen a steamy yarn about a nymphomaniac mega-model. It just kind of happened. Something I started scrawling as a lark during film class careened way beyond my control.

Maybe I was an oversexed gorgeous Swede with naturally humungous breasts in my past life. Inga just flowed out of me. She was an uneducated poor girl from a little Swedish village with not much to offer save for what she thought were her most marketable assets: that healthy-sized chest, exceptionally high cheekbones, and pouty lips that were put to productive use at a very early age. No one was able to gather enough evidence, but what the local papers referred to as "the Sauerkraut Scandal" (an incident town folk whisper had to do with mayor, shredded cabbage, and mystery meat) seemed to trigger Inga's hasty departure from the little hamlet. She hit Paris and the best boudoirs along the Seine. Soon her pelvis required medical attention, but her "connections" helped pave the way for her to become a modeling superstar. She eventually had a string of husbands—including an impotent baron—before settling in L.A. where she married Chuck Woolery and was a semi-regular on *Falcon Crest*. Okay so *Inga* might be the most ridiculously amateurish story ever told, but I still made sure Inga had her happy ending (or at least my twisted version of one).

• • •

Shari went to junior college with me, and she became the president of my book club. At first, I wrote *Inga* to amuse and entertain her. But she became riveted. Obsessed. She egged me on, telling me, "This is better than Jackie Collins," which was a huge compliment, since Jackie Collins pretty much owned the Vixen-Fellating-Her-Way-to-the-Top genre. She began passing the chapters around the cafeteria and other people read it and asked for more. *Inga* was soon everywhere.

Becoming an overnight pseudo-literary sensation certainly helped my self-esteem. Kind of like micro-dermabrasion for the psyche, the acceptance blasted away at the scars puberty had inflicted on me. Through slutty, insatiable Inga, I found my own slutty, insatiable voice. People started to "get" my wacky personality.

Alas, my clothes had not quite caught up with my new, creative life. The singer **Prince** had exploded onto the scene and I liked what I saw. Ruffles on a guy? Jumpsuits with peek-aboo panels? It was all so daring, so rock-star, so me (at least in my head). But I just couldn't keep up with this hyper-hip musical elf, or the other pop stars at the time, like Madonna, Billy Idol, or Janet Jackson. Money was tight, so I had to make a choice: college or clothes. Clothes had the edge, but then my dad said I would be disowned and would have to wash dishes at the Ben Ash Delicatessen to support myself. I elected to save myself from scrubbing gefilte fish off plates and reluctantly opted for a higher education.

I did manage to put together one passably glamorous outfit:

Shari and me after she nobly adopted me as her pet charity project
(Shari Isenberg)

a pair of skin-tight gray Levi corduroys, a dark gray Ralph Lauren sweater (my attempt to keep up with Ralph queen Shari), and ode-to-Prince gray suede platform boots. But what was a necessary height lift to the pint-size pop star was, in retrospect, ghastly on tall and gangly me. Think of Lurch with a wiggle and you get the less-than-gorgeous picture.

From Dawson College, I went on to Concordia University and felt like I was in a Fellini movie. It was as if all the outcasts in the world had suddenly taken over, and the world didn't fall apart in the process. My professors were these bohemian types who debated me and encouraged me to be as much of a freak as I wanted to be. They kept telling me I had an "interesting mind," which made me feel like they wanted to dissect my frontal lobes as a fact-finding lab experiment. But now I see it was just their way of complimenting and respecting me. I had gotten so used to being an outsider that I needed a little bit of an adjustment period. I had to ask, "You mean I'm not the freak du jour anymore?" It's still a question I ask myself sometimes.

University had its moments, but I was absolutely itching to get into the real world. The frat house parties, drinking beer—

all of that bored me. If you'd asked me then what I wanted to be, I would have said: rock star or jet-setter, assuming you could jet-set full time with benefits. I was so wildly attracted to that lifestyle, and I knew it wasn't make-believe.

These days people often ask me, "Where did you come from? How did you happen?" I flash back on this period of my life. If any dreamers-disguised-as-misfits are reading this right now, I was one of you. I dreamed so hard that my head hurt. I'm very pro-dreaming because I had a lot of spirit smashers and negative people in my life.

Even my loving dad could burst my bubble. Dad is a very realistic, practical person and he would often tell me, "Stop dreaming. Get your head out of the clouds. There's a real world out there and one day you're going to have to pay rent and function." Ugh, how mundane.

I'm very pro-dreaming because I had a lot of spirit smashers and negative people in my life.

Practically speaking, you can even get your career going long before you've found your official adult hairstyle. When I was sixteen, I got my first article published in the *Montreal Gazette* about the importance of men's cologne. It was a very big deal—this was the *New York Times* of Montreal. I interviewed the city's top media movers and shakers and I asked them what their favorite cologne was. I got paid a whopping fifty dollars for it. I went straight out and bought a bottle of Santos by Cartier cologne with it. I figured smelling expensive was a good career move.

• • •

I put myself through college working at the Saidye Bronfman Centre. It was a cultural center with an art school, theater, and gallery, and I was the nighttime receptionist. I was terrible at it. I would drop calls constantly; there are probably still people I put on hold. I never knew the correct answer to anything. People would call and ask, "Can you tell me about the ceramics class? What kind of clay do they use?" And I'd say "Play-Doh."

But I turned the Saidye Bronfman Centre into my stage. I really did *like* yapping on the phone, and I would really connect with shut-ins who yearned for some kind of contact with the outside world. The center also had the only Yiddish theater in Canada, and the woman who ran it— Dora Wasserman, a fiery Russian woman who looked like **Ozzy Osbourne** in drag—put me into one of her plays. I thought I should approach this with the Method acting style, so in my head I pretended that I was an edgy **Mickey Rourke** thrown into a turn-of-the-century peasant village, kind of like *9 1/2 Weeks* meets *Yentl*, if you will. Unfortunately, Steven/Mickey didn't know how to speak Yiddish. I had to learn my part phonetically. The play turned out to be a hit and ran for four months. I loved every night. It was Broadway to me. Dora eventually told me that I was a lousy actor— and I was—but that I had energy enough for fifty people.

Now that I was starting to get a profile, I wanted to change my clunky, unpronounceable surname. For the record, the best way to pronounce it is to split it in two and take the phonetic approach: COJO—pause—CARU. I thought Cojo-pause-caru made a statement in print, but it sounded to me like the name of a vicious venereal disease indigenous to the outskirts of Bulgaria when said out loud. Of course, I was teased about it constantly. Some sample comic riffs on my name (courtesy of so-called friends): Steven Guadalajara, Steven Cojagoogoo, Steven Kangaroo, and my personal favorite, Steven-cut-your-cock-off. For someone who wanted to be Americanized so badly, this bizarre Romanian moniker—actually a very common name heard in the best torture chambers in Transylvania—was my worst nightmare. So I picked up a legal pad and came up with a list of slicker-sounding names. *Dynasty* was my life at that point, so soap-opera names came pouring from my brain: Steven Dalton, Steven Nolan, Steven Drake, Steven Alexander, and Steven Baron. I also considered adding a *Von* in the middle to sound regal. (Can you imagine Katie or Matt introducing me as Steven Von Cojocaru with a straight face?) But eventually everything sounded pale in comparison to *Cojocaru*, which means, by the way, "leather tanner" in Romanian. Rather fitting these days since I'm really in touch with my ethnicity and my leather.

As far as I was concerned, I had landed the biggest job in showbiz. Barely out of university, I was hired as a talent booker for a local telethon and my mission was to book an American star to headline the night. The pressure was on. I felt like I was booking the Oscars. I approached my producer and said, "What about **Cher**, **Olivia Newton-John**, **George Michael**, **Dolly Parton**, **Barbra Streisand** all singing 'Kumbaya' in

French?" He looked back me and said, "You're dreaming in Technicolor. If you get Suzanne Somers to do belly dance while humming the *Three's Company* theme song, you'll get a bonus."

Everybody watched the telethon channel, Montreal's CFCF-12. This was a big deal. We had to land somebody with a name, a profile, who wasn't above renting their fame to a random cause for twenty-four hours. A lot of people look at these charity events and think stars do it out of the goodness of their heart. Well, we *paid* our big headliners fifteen thousand dollars, flew them in first class, and put them up at the Ritz-Carlton.

My first industry job taught me a harsh lesson: It's not all glamour. In between searching for our star, I had to book the middle-of-the-night block of the telethon. I was deeply bothered by Shoshanna and her troupe of Israeli folk dancers who agreed to perform at 3:30 A.M. I was angry that me, Mr. Hollywood of Canada, was reduced to dealing with a group that clearly was a million miles away from the Go-Gos. Worse, the emerging glamour boy in me couldn't relate to these *au naturel* girls who didn't shave their legs. I thought this was a crime worthy of permanent exile to a kibbutz.

When it came to the big American star, I had a list and I called all the big agencies: William Morris, ICM, CAA. I would sit at my desk in the basement of CFCF-12's headquarters and try to sound like a fast-talking showbiz veteran when I got a William Morris biggie on the line.

"Hi, this is Steven Cojocaru at CFCF-12. I'd like to book the Rolling Stones to do a big gig here." After countless clicks, desperation got the better of me and I changed my tune to something much more to the point: "Hi. Who wants to do a one-nighter in Montreal and get in some good shopping, too?"

Somehow, I managed to book the singer **Laura Branigan**.

I am the journalism equivalent of a cheese soufflé.

Her big hit, "Gloria," had come and gone and her career was less than sizzling, but I became the hero for landing her. I swooned when she showed up with her whole entourage—an assistant, a musical director, and her manager. I thought, "Oh. My God. A famous person. I guess they get to have slaves." But she was really nice to me in that fake, Hollywood, You're-My-New-Favorite-Person way. We all went out for dinner and I was beyond starstruck.

Laura worked really hard for the bucks. During her performance, she sang live along with a recording of "Gloria." But something happened to the sound system, and the tape got stuck and just kept playing the "Gloria" chorus over and over and over. It just kept going and Laura was such a pro that she kept singing. We must have used up an hour of telethon time on that one song. The pledge money rolled in.

I am the journalism equivalent of a cheese soufflé. I was born to be fluffy. And in Canada, we had this national fashion magazine called *Flare,* a sort of *InStyle* of the North. After the telethon, I started working for them and covering parties for a column in *Flare* called "Flare Was There."

It was the perfect job for me: getting paid to be a professional gadabout. I covered the Montreal World Film Festival when **Clint Eastwood** and **Jane Fonda** were there. I met **Luciano Pavarotti** and I was trembling. My headline? "Something in the Aria." (I loved puns. For that piece I wrote, "Luciano sang with such drama and pain that it threatened to become the 'Opera Winfrey Show.' ") It was a revelation seeing people smartly turned out in tuxedos and gowns and serious baubles. Certainly, this was a long way from the bar mitzvah circuit with nary a discounted marabou-feather-trimmed caftan in sight. These assignments and stars just got bigger and bigger. I interviewed the former prime minister of Canada, Pierre Trudeau, who was a legend in Canada and a very dashing, elegant man—like a Canadian Matt Lauer. I wasn't bad at idle chitchat. I honed my basic interview skills and learned not to attack famous people and ask them questions like, "Do you shoot up in your spare time?" I was much better at discussing their favorite lipstick shades anyway.

I was as shocked as anyone to suddenly discover I was clairvoyant. Okay, I couldn't really predict impending stock market crashes, but I was okay at being a phony psychic for hire. I had a friend, Karen Evans, who was one of the cohosts of a wacky radio show in Montreal, and she thought I was odd and good radio material. She said, "I'd like you to call in once in a while. Why don't you think of a character?" I decided to be a psychic to the stars called "Mystic Pizza." I called up the show and said that I was in a limo with **Geena Davis** and I was giving her a bikini wax while touching her forehead for vibrations. On the air, we had a séance to try to bring back **Demi Moore**'s dead dog,

Gigi. And when Gigi came back, he had a message for Demi: "Don't wear bicycle pants to the Oscars." Smart pooch.

Both hosts of the show were jumping in and we had a great back-and-forth. So I wrote more skits, and they got more and more wild. I did one where I told the listeners that **Nancy Reagan**'s eyebrows were communicating with me and that they were like Nostradamus and were predicting World War III. Soon enough, it started to get around Montreal that I was "Mystic Pizza" and people knew my voice. To this day I look back on that gig so fondly. It allowed me to go really out there and show my personality. Everybody needs an outlet. That was mine.

Through all these little exposures—the telethon, the job at *Flare,* and "Mystic Pizza"—I met up with Andy Nulman, the clever nutjob who cofounded the Montreal Just for Laughs Comedy Festival. Andy changed my life by letting me fail.

Andy was like me: a wacky, nice Jewish boy. He made me the director of public relations for the comedy festival even though I had as much experience as a fifteen-year-old intern. This was a huge job; I had to help design the entire publicity campaign. I had to book comics on interviews. I met dozens of Hollywood producers looking for talent and comics from around the world. I saw the masters and the duds, like Jingo: The Guy Who Puts a Firecracker Up His Bum and Lights It.

But I had a fatal flaw as a publicist—I was obsessed with my appearance. Primping was my real full-time vocation. I'd spend hours trying to tame my wild curly hair, and figuring out which boots would go with which jeans. I began to be late for every meeting and every event. I would have to show up and drive a comic to a radio station for an interview, and Oops! I was an hour late because I was too busy struggling with the round brush.

Andy, on my last day of work, invited me into his office. He told me he had some good news and some bad news. The bad news—point blank—was that I sucked as a publicist. I was disorganized, ditzy, and had no organizational skills whatsoever. The good news, he said, was that I was a born clown and I should be in front of the camera. "You shouldn't be promoting other people," he told me. "You should be on television."

That was a conversation that changed my life. Andy gave me confidence when I didn't have any. I looked up to him as Mr. Mega-Plugged In. At that moment when I was just this live wire of ambition and had dreams that were all over the map, Andy put my story together for me.

By this time, I had my own place in Montreal. I thought having my own pied-à-terre all the way downtown would satisfy my living large urges—even if it was just a studio the size of a box a pair of Jimmy Choos comes in. It was in a doorman building and just a stone's throw from bustling St. Catherine Street. But after Andy Nulman's speech, all I could think about was Hollywood and my desperation to get there.

It took my college friend Tobie Rozaklis to actually get me out of Montreal and onto my first red carpet.

Tobie was an extremely bright six-foot-tall glamazon who

was all about the big picture. Her parents were struggling Greek immigrants. It was the Old World parents versus the New World kid scenario I knew all too well. She wanted to get to Hollywood as much as I did. I knew Hollywood like the back of my hand—I had devoured every article, every celebrity biography—but Tobie had the moxie to get us there.

She'd been to L.A. once as a freelance radio reporter. When she came back, she said to me, "Steven, I went to the Grammys and next year you're coming with me." I said, "Tobie— don't say that. I can barely breathe." But she was adamant. The next year, when the Grammys came around, we forged press credentials as representatives from this big radio station in Montreal where Tobie had a friend. With our bogus letterhead, we blew all our savings on airplane tickets and headed to Glamourville.

After we landed, Tobie took me straight to Santa Monica behind the wheel of our rented royal blue Ford Taurus. It was so warm and bright, I had trouble dilating my pupils after a childhood in cold, rainy Montreal. I picked up on the hedonism quick—seeing girls Roller-Blading in bikinis on the boardwalk and tanned guys with shaggy hair speeding down the streets in their Porsche convertibles. Then Tobie turned to me and asked, "Do you want to go the short way or the long way to our hotel?" I had no idea how to get there, so I shrugged. Tobie said, "I think you want to go the long way," and smiled. She drove us along Sunset Boulevard, all the way from the beach to Beverly Hills. I had goose bumps on top of goose bumps. I had been imagining this landscape for so long, and now I was here, in the zip code of my fantasy life. Winding foothill roads. Palm trees. A hair salon on practically every corner. I took to Vapid City immediately. We came to an intersection in front of the Beverly Hills Hotel and a car pulled up next to us: a vintage Roadster with a Robert Redford type driving and his blond, buxom girlfriend in the passenger seat. Two perfect Hollywood people in a perfectly cinematic moment. Honestly, I flatlined.

Our hotel was behind the swank Beverely Wilshire Hotel— in fact, our home away from home had been the posh hotel's maids' quarters at one time. It was a dump, but it was in 90210 and that's all that mattered. That afternoon, we walked to Rodeo Drive. I thought it would be a gigantic castle with stores in the courtyard. I had imagined that there would be outdoor chandeliers and a swimming pool in the middle of the street with **Donna Mills** topless on a chaise lounge. I was disappointed—it was just a street with outrageously expensive stores.

Take-charge Tobie bought us a star map and we decided to drive to **Johnny Carson**'s house in Malibu. We didn't get to traipse through Casa Carson. We got as far as the imposing wrought-iron gate. Beside the Keep Out or Die! gate was a little mailbox, and tons of security cameras. This was good enough for me. I leaped out of the car and slowly caressed Johnny Carson's iron bars. My pumped-up reaction was not far from that of an eight-year-old girl getting to touch **Justin Timberlake**'s used napkin—I started jumping up and down, saying, "I touched Johnny's gate! I touched Johnny's gate!" I wanted so badly to open the correspondence peeking out of the mailbox.

But Tobie talked me down, saying that it was a federal crime and that all the cameras would capture me doing it. And I said. "Forget it. My hair doesn't look good enough to be on camera."

The next day was Grammys day. Tobie was calm but I was practically convulsing. I spent the better part of the day blowing and gelling and re-blowing my hair. Finally it was a poufy, if unmovable, masterpiece.

Then out of the closet came the artillery: My ultimate late-1980s ensemble starring an electric-blue wool blazer with black stripes, which boasted shoulder pads so enormous, one could have balanced sterling silver hors d'oeuvres trays on them. Underneath, I wore a white raw-silk shirt and black baggy trousers. I thought it was a terribly sophisticated look, but I probably looked more like the makeup man on the M. C. Hammer tour.

As Tobie steered the Taurus in front of the Shrine Auditorium, I laid my eyes on the Garden of Eden. Before me was the red carpet at last. In my mind, I thought it was an endless path that perhaps floated off to heaven. But this was really an extended welcome mat thrown on top of a sidewalk. And the luminous glow that always bounced off of it on TV was in person a battery of harsh Klieg lights about as friendly to the eye as mall lights. But it was the crowd who brought it to life. The Anointed Ones with their perfect smiles, glossy—read "unfrizzy"—hair, and high glam clothes. I felt flushed. I was home.

Or so I thought. Tobie drove right past the red carpet. "Where are you going?" I shrieked. Then she dropped the bomb: "We're not credentialed for the red carpet," she said. She then lowered her eyes and informed me that bottom-of-the-totem-pole reporters went through the back of the auditorium and straight to the press room. To add insult to injury, we had to park fifteen blocks away and grab a shuttle over to the site. "My shoulder pads will never fit into that thing," I barked at Tobie who shoved me inside the minivan anyway.

So I lied when I told everyone back home that I had tickets to the Grammys. What I really had was a fold-up picnic chair next to someone from Bombay TV. But I did get to see *everyone*. Every time a star won an award, they were shepherded backstage, where there was a little microphone and platform set up for them. The press pack sat squeezed together and peppered each star with questions. I heard that **Barbra Streisand** had won a Grammy and was headed backstage. It couldn't be that in a few minutes BARBRA, who in the Jewish community was considered a near religious figure, would be standing before me. My mother prayed to her. The main educational moment in my family was not *National Geographic*, but my mom sitting me down in front of *Funny Girl* on television with a look on her face that said, "You will be quizzed on this afterward."

I might have had all the color drained from my face when BARBRA appeared a few feet in front of me, but she looked great: porcelain skin and cute petite frame. The nose even didn't look that big. She was curt with people, Yes, No, very black and white. I had heard a rumor that she was going to record "Somewhere Over the Rainbow," and I built up all my courage to ask her a question. "Barbra—Barbra" I said, voice cracking like a twelve-year-old boy, "Steven Cojocaru, CJAD

Radio Montreal." And she said, "Hiii . . ." in that Brooklynese twang. "Is it true," I asked, "that you're thinking about recording 'Somewhere Over the Rainbow'?" And she smiled and answered, "Actually, no, I was thinking about it, but . . ." Clearly, she liked my question because she just babbled on and on.

I wasn't listening to a word. Here I was backstage at the Grammys, on a first-name basis with the Dalai Lama of Jewish Life, in the city of my childhood dreams. I could barely recognize my life.

I almost tinkled in the slightly damaged markdown Calvin Klein drawers my mother bought me.

FOUR

1001 ROMANIAN SLANG WORDS FOR "HOOKER"

D id Barbra Streisand emit subliminal messages to yours truly? I could swear she was communicating telepathically with me at the Grammys and saying "Move to L.A., bubaleh." I didn't argue. Back in Montreal, Mom reacted to my announcement that I was packing up my collection of leather pants and hightailing it to Hollywood with the kind of dignified restraint I expected of her. "I'm having a stroke," she yelled between loud sucking gasps for air.

Then, summoning all the strength her ninty-nine-pound body could muster, she served up a high-pitched soliloquy on the evils of this palm tree–dotted Sodom and Gomorrah. After listening to forty-five minutes about hashish junkies and hearing 1001 Romanian slang words for "hooker," I suggested she come with me to L.A. and pay the rent by writing sordid teenage runaway teleflicks. Fuming, my sweet, normally nonviolent mother said she would have socked me in the mouth if she hadn't paid for my orthodontia bills. *Touché.*

I was so possessed by the pull L.A. had on me, I had very

little fear about moving to a city where I barely knew any-one. It was all systems go until me and the family stood at the departure gate at Montreal's Dorval Airport. Seeing my ashen-faced parents so raw with pain destroyed me. It was group sob time and I was quickly losing my nerve. I was sud-denly a little tyke again, and all I wanted was for my mom to make me a hot chocolate and for us to have a chitchat about Elizabeth Taylor's diamond drop earrings. But my noble parents, always putting my needs above theirs, literally pushed me toward the airplane and a giant step closer to my dreams.

The Oakwood Apartments was where I decided to hang my chapeau. I had read about these short-stay corporate resi-dences littered throughout L.A. and figured I could camp there until I a) married money or b) got a talk show. I gave myself about six weeks to accomplish either. I picked the Oakwood's Burbank location because it was across the street from Warner Brothers Studios and was where the studio put up out-of-town talent. I ignored all the red flags at first. Okay, so the row upon row of identical mini-buildings with their sterile facades looked like campus housing. Surely they were saving the property's lone VIP Mediterranean villa just for me.

I was wrong. My new home was about the size of a Louis Vuitton weekend bag with fluorescent lights and a hot plate. Well, at least I had cable and better still, free adult channels. I was actually quite entertained (all right, maybe even titillated) by the stereophonic moans and groans until I realized the tele-vision wasn't even on. The "Oh, Jim, oh, Sue, oh, Jim" refrains were being beamed live from the other side of the tissue-thin walls. Despite going to sleep every night with a pillow over my head and my TV blasting, I wasn't spared from finding out that Sue had a seemingly insatiable oral fixation and that Jim cottoned to being called Captain.

I was so demented and delusional that I went to the complex's swimming pool every day—if I was good at anything it was an artful lounging pose—convinced that I would get discovered by a sunbathing producer. I believed that that if I read *Variety* by the pool every day for six weeks, I would have a talk show. But the six weeks turned into a year—subsidized by my parents—of lying by the pool and no show. All I got was a wicked sunburn. I looked like a rejected California raisin.

I did venture out occasionally to feed my obsessive star lust. I made the pilgrimage to Westward Memorial Park, where Marilyn Monroe is buried. I hit rigor mortis paydirt when I saw how chic her grave site is. Marilyn is interred in a wall, like a vault. It's marble with an elegant less-is-more plaque that simply reads, "Marilyn Monroe 1926 to 1962." I was immediately struck with the thought that it's not a bad idea to have a style game-plan from birth to the afterlife. Marilyn knew this. Except that in so many ways, she was not savvy. I decided we needed to have a heartfelt talk about practical matters. So in the middle of the cemetery, I start yapping to the wall, er, Marilyn. I said, "Why did you mess around with the Kennedys? Those boys were trouble. If you hadn't

All I got was a wicked sunburn. I looked like a rejected California raisin.

fooled around with the Kennedy boys you would be alive and well and starring on *Knots Landing* now."

That jaunt inspired me to do more hobnobbing with glamorous dead stars. After consulting my star map, I decided I had to pay Joan Crawford a visit. I had devoured *Mommie Dearest* and read about her mansion in Brentwood. It sounded like the very height of Old Hollywood sophistication, and in my mind this was a journey akin to trekking to the Taj Mahal. So I found my way to Bristol Avenue and Miss Crawford's front gate. I tried to climb over the wall, and the house caretaker caught me and barked, "What are you doing here?"

"I really want to see Joan Crawford's house," I stammered. He took pity on me. He winked and said, "I can't let you into the house, but I'll give you a special treat. Why don't you come with me to the back of the house and I'll show you the pool." Thinking back, it sounds to me like a come-on line from a NAMBLA member, but back then it was the opportunity of a lifetime (and thankfully a genuine act of kindness). The pool was gigantic. This was a complete Hollywood movie-star life. Scenes like this—getting special access, seeing celebrity life up close—really fed me.

After seeing Crawford's digs, I knew it was time to ditch the Oakwood (and regrettably Sue and Jim) and get myself a geographically desirable address. Beverly Hills, of course. I thought if I lived at the right address, my career would skyrocket. I got the local Beverly Hills newspaper, the *Courier*, and looked up the rentals there. I thought, "Four hundred dollars is pretty much my maximum rent, so maybe I can afford to live in a guest house of a mansion." That would be perfect: dirt-cheap but sort of near real glamour.

The ad was my dream come true: a fully-furnished guest house on Weatherly Drive. I had an immediate vision of a charming Cape Cod–style cottage set among manicured lawns that went on forever. But when I drove up to the property and looked at the main house, I was disappointed to find a smallish, very-average family abode. An elderly woman named Bertha flung open the door. She couldn't have been nicer—an all-smiles chubby-cheeked Jewish woman from Poland who lived there with her retired husband Sol. The wheels in my devious mind starting turning. Play up the nice-Jewish-boy thing, I told myself, and I'd be getting five-course meals—I like my filet mignon on the medium side, Auntie Bertha—and my skivvies pressed on a daily basis. Maybe even a Godiva chocolate placed on my pillow every night too. Bertha instantly bathed me in love. Within minutes, she was calling me darling and taking me by the hand to the "adorable" guesthouse. "Bertha, this looks like a converted garage," I said. "Garage, schmarage," she pooh-poohed. "It's a *Beverly Hills* guest house. I have a waiting list for it." She opened the door and we fell into the black hole of hell. It was a minuscule room with a lone sliver of a window and a few pieces of rickety furniture from the Bates Motel school of decor. Attached was a demi-bathroom with a shower stall about as roomy as a Fed Ex envelope. But I was desperate. I didn't have enough money for a big security deposit on a real apartment and no furniture of my own. I fooled myself into believing that I'd be okay with a Beverly Hills address and manipulating Bertha into being my lady-in-waiting.

But I was an amateur con artist next to the Bonnie and Clyde of Warsaw. Once I moved in, Bertha and Sol dropped the foster-grandparents act and showed their real, conniving, slumlord selves. Shifty and Smarmy, as I soon took to calling them under my breath, never told me my prison cell was unheated or that I'd be showering with brown water.

They never invited me into their home, except when Bertha needed something done. She had a pacemaker and she couldn't lift things or climb. I had to put her chicken in the microwave for her—she was "too weak." Finally, I'm ashamed to admit, I started to plot Bertha's assassination. I would lie in my cot and think about casually running a refrigerator magnet across her pacemaker the next time I was "helping" her with defrosting.

After eight months of this torture, I came up with an escape plan. It was time to swallow my pride and call in the big guns to spring me: My parents. I invited them to come visit. When my mom walked into the hovel, she burst into tears. Dad pulled out his checkbook. They gave me enough money for a deposit on a new apartment, a bed, and a television. I fled Weatherly Drive a few days later.

For the first five years I was in Los Angeles, every agent and producer I met told me, "Pack it in. I think you have more of a chance of being a paratrooper than being on television." They said, "You're too flamboyant." So I was stuck bottom-feeding. I worked for **Richard Moll**'s publicist in the early 1990s. Richard

Those who can, act. Those who can't are relegated to stamping Richard Moll's 8 x 10 glossies. *(©Bettmann/CORBIS)*

had been a big star on *Night Court*, and I was an assistant for his publicist. At first, he wanted me to keep his receipts organized. But when he saw how useless I was at that, he gave me the worst job possible: He had me sign Richard Moll's autographs for him. He had Richard's signature made on a stamp and I spent all day stamping his eight-by-ten glossies. There. You have it. A big confession. I never met Richard, but I read his fan mail and it was amazing. Everybody loved him and they were so gushy about how he made them laugh. I would sit, put my feet up on the desk, and waste the day reading these fan letters, fantasizing that the mail was for me.

By 1994 I was doing public relations for a Beverly Hills publicist who had this weird list of clients: **Victoria Jackson**, not the comic, but the infomercial makeup queen, and **Jack Pedota**, an artist who did the poster for the *Batman* movie. One day we took a *People* magazine reporter named Nancy Matsumoto to lunch to sell her on Jack as a "story"—he'd been **Tim Burton**'s pizza delivery boy. But at the lunch, Nancy was more impressed by the *People* magazine database in my head than she was by Jack's story. She could throw out a name, like **Victoria Principal**, and I'd give you her whole bio and credits and who she schtupped in 1981 in a hot tub. I was a living, breathing version of *People.*

At the same time, on the side, I was writing a column for this hipster L.A. magazine called *Bang!* The column was titled "The Young and the Guest List," and it opened lots of doors for me because I was out all the time, meeting Young Hollywood. I remember going to cover this fund-raiser for AIDS Project Los Angeles at the Shrine Auditorium, that included a fashion show for **Jean Paul Gaultier**. **Madonna** starred in the fashion show (He's one of her favorite designers.) and for the grand finale, Madonna came out topless. This was a lot for my innocent little Montreal peepers, but everybody else was in shock too. I raced home to tell my mom, "I saw Madonna's breasts!" She answered, "Get on the next bus home! You're being corrupted!"

My first big assignment almost destroyed my budding career. I was at Chasen's—the classic post-Oscars haunt on Beverly Boulevard—for the premiere party of the movie *Sommersby*. I was covering it for *Us* magazine. I was completely green—this was my first time behind Hollywood's A-list velvet rope into one of the most fabled joints in the city. Everything was exactly how I had envisioned it: dark mahogany and sexy leather booths and **Claudia Schiffer**.

At that moment, Claudia was the scorching-hot über model. She hit the party with some girlfriends, but wasn't without male company for long. I stood beside Claudia because I wanted to be a fly on her wall. A seemingly endless army of salivating industry types came over to hit on her. Schiffer did not seem all that skilled at handling cheesy players. She did a lot of giggling but appeared awkward and out of her element. A round and troll-like producer came up to her and said, "Claudia, you must come out to the beach this weekend for an audition." She just blushed and said, "Sure." We were both too innocent then to decode Mr. Short and Stubby's real message: "Come out to my Malibu beach house and get ready to road test my new penile implant."

But I wasn't there to talk to Claudia—**Richard Gere**, who costarred in *Sommersby* with **Jodie Foster**, was the real star in the room. His publicist arranged a minute for me to talk to him. At one point in the 1980s I wanted to be Richard Gere. I wanted to be the American Gigolo and drive the black Mercedes in an Armani wardrobe. So I started hyperventilating. My marching orders had been to get light, fun quotes, and not do a dissertation about cinema or the political system in Tibet.

So I asked him, "What was it like to kiss **Jodie Foster**?"

I should have known better. It was like I was from *Teen Beat*. He blew up and walked away in a huff. I was heartbroken. And *Us* magazine never used me again.

• • •

Things were getting rough. I just wasn't making enough money to get by. I had a four-hundred-dollar phone bill and the phone company was threatening to cut off my service. Then they did. Then my electricity got cut off. That stinging poverty stays with you. To this day when I plug in my flat iron, I'm always like, "Take a breath. Will there be electricity?" My friends, though, took pity on me. They bailed me out countless times. Like Abby—my first friend in L.A.—who would write me a check for $200 and tell me to "go buy some groceries and pay some bills." Or my friend Shane, who bought some of my leather and suede jackets from me because he knew I needed the money. Not the best arrangement, though, considering that after the leather sale Shane, better known as the "Rogue with the Brogue," would want to go barhopping, and I'd blow my newfound score on Heinekins.

So, in desperation, I took a job at Disney. You're not called "employees" at Disney—you're called "cast members." Everything is referred to in hyper-cheery Disney terms, like, "Have a Mickey Mouse Day." But I wasn't buying it. I showed up to work with my hair slicked back into a ponytail and wearing one earring like I was a Peruvian drug lord. I had to show how different I was. Take that, Pluto.

I was supposed to be at Disney as a temp, but then a miracle happened: I found an adopted family and a long-term day job. I reported to work that first day with a sinking feeling that I had been sucked into a cult of lifeless white-bread-eating zombies. I was pretty much on the money except for Barbara and Doris. Barbara Kasadra-Black and Doris Beard were my supervisors. At first glance, Barbara was public enemy number one. I pegged her as the ultimate priss who probably wore her sensible shoes and white turtleneck in the shower. I wrote off Doris, too—anyone who crunched numbers was too Establishment for my nonconformist tastes. But beyond their oh-so-respectable masks were two of the most colorful and loving people I've ever had the good fortune to know. Behind closed doors, they put down their flow charts and we dished and dished. But keep that quiet, I don't want to blow their covers.

I was there for two years. One of my duties was to inspect the stuffed animals to do quality control. But I was so busy day-dreaming about Hollywood, everything instantly passed inspection. There are probably Goofys out there with amputed tails and missing eyes thanks to me. Sorry, kids. (Just kidding—thankfully, the toys had to go on to pass more inspections.)

Then another miracle happened. "Steven, you should come work for the magazine." It was Nancy Matsumoto calling from *People*. She had decided that I should interview for a job with *People*'s Los Angeles office bureau chief. At that point, I wasn't sure what I could really contribute. There was just this irregular fashion page that they did, maybe once a month. That was the only thing I was attracted to.

I went to meet the bureau chief, and he was very cordial.

The way you start at *People* magazine is you start at the bottom, one of four or five people whose names are listed at the end of an article, and climb up the ladder. He said I would start at the bottom rung. I was very open to that, but I was adamant about one thing.

To say that I started "at the bottom" is a compliment. I was submailroom.

"I love Hollywood and fashion," I said. "That fashion page you do is my area. Can I work for that page?"

He gave me some fatherly advice. "You know, fashion is not really big with the magazine," he said. "It's not really a priority. There's more of a need for general entertainment reporters."

I wouldn't budge. I wanted to be on that page.

To say that I started "at the bottom" is a compliment. I was submailroom. I was what is affectionately known as a "stringer," which is somewhere between a slave and a sanitation engineer. They call you when they have extra work because everybody else is busy and doesn't care. You have no rights, no benefits. You're invisible. But it was *People* magazine.

My first article was about **Tom Ford**'s arrival at Gucci. Five people "wrote" this article, and I contributed one sentence:

"When you see Tom's things," says actress Jennifer Tilly, a fan, "there's an almost uncontrollable 'I've got to have it' feeling."

As a stringer, you just gather the quotes and send them to the editors, who make the prose all pretty. You don't get to write anything. I got the Jennifer Tilly quote. Still, to me, this was a gigantic accomplishment. This was my start. At the same time, I knew I didn't want to be a full-time journalist. It wasn't nearly flashy or glam enough for me. You can't just call it in when you're a journalist—there has to be a serious side to what you do. I was too raw and wild. I wanted to go to parties and be crazy.

But that was perfect for the "Stylewatch" section, because most of the quotes for that section came from parties. If you're doing a story on the new Hollywood moms, all the reporters get orders that whatever party you go to, if you see celebrities, ask them what it's like to be a new mom. That's how it works. And nobody was going to more parties than me.

I got good at extraction. I would go to movie premieres with no intention of writing about the movie. I was trying to get face-time with celebrities. It worked like this: I would arrange to talk to, say, **Johnny Depp**. Sure, I would fall asleep when he told me about his method acting and how he got into the mind-set of playing a chair. My eyes would glaze over and I would start to think about my laundry, mentally separating the darks from the lights, but then I would slip in the completely unrelated question: Who are you dating? Are you a member of the Mile-high Club? By doing this, I met everybody.

1996 VH1 AWARDS
Shrine Auditorium, Downtown Los Angeles

If dressing like an alien worked for David Bowie, it was good enough for me. I was off to a major rock awards fête and was determined to be noticed. I had the flash of the Space Oddity persona David Bowie had so glamorously and bizarrely affected in the 1970s. Yup, that's it. I would become a Bowie-esque dazzling space creature for the night. I had a designer friend who instantly got the vision. Ground Control to Major Tom—here comes Steven in a skintight, white-rubber jumpsuit and matching white platform boots.

My mode of transportation at the time was a barely breathing mid-1980s model gray Chevrolet Cavalier. I was in such denial about this wildly embarrassing jalopy, I'd put on dark glasses and pretend I was driving a Mercedes. I never got it serviced. I

Even at Midas, you are what you drive in LA.

didn't want to experience the humiliation of bringing it to a mechanic. Even at Midas, you are what you drive in L.A. Just before the VH-1 event, the Cavalier was starting to gasp for air and was chug-a-lugging all the time. These were clearly wailing cries for help. But I completely ignored them and chose to spend the money on shoes. Shallow is as shallow does.

The space creature was behind the wheel and driving on the freeway to Downtown L.A. when the Cavalier started coughing uncontrollably. I kept driving, trying to hold out so I could at least make it to the Shrine. All the while, I chanted a silent prayer: "Please let me get to valet parking and get out of this heap so I can be David Bowie for the night."

It was limo gridlock in front of the Shrine. Me and the Cav were in line with the gleaming chariots. Come on Cavalier, hold on for just another minute. KABOOM. Smoke was filling up the inside of the car. I jumped out to see green liquid spraying from under the hood and forming a gooey layer all over the now-comatose automobile. Horns were blaring. Limo drivers screaming. I wanted to disappear. It's not easy blending when you look like a giant Q-Tip. My public hanging was slow and deliberate. Someone rolled down their car window. "Steven, is that you? Is that your car?" Sirens were blasting through my eardrums. Am I dead yet? Maybe the big white light of death is really a red flashing light. Two police officers were now in my face. "Move your car. You're backing up traffic for miles." David Bowie would never have to endure this.

Being a freak never had such a downside. The police abandoned me to direct traffic around the car. I had no cell phone. I was forced to flee on foot to the USC campus across the street in search of a pay phone. I just surrendered to the humiliation of looking like a cross-dressing version of the Good Humor Man as frat boys stopped in their tracks to stare and titter.

I called a tow truck, and with the beaten-down Martian sitting in the truck with a guy named Bubba, we dragged my poor, destroyed car to a garage in the heart of the 'hood. I had to stand outside while the mechanic gave the Cavalier a complete hysterectomy. While I was trying to calm down and pretend this nightmare wasn't really happening, a souped-up old

Cadillac convertible stopped at the traffic light a few feet away from me. A bunch of sinister looking teens were in the car. They looked at me, and then the final flogging happened. They started whistling at me and one guy screamed out, "Hey, are you Michael Jackson?"

At this point, spooning with a chimp inside a hyperbaric chamber sounded appealing.

———m———

CANNES—BRIGITTE, SOPHIA, AND MR. SPINDLY LEGS

May 1998

Airport terminal, Nice, France

Where else but the French Riviera can you stroll off of an airplane and be greeted by **Brigitte Bardot** striking a sex-kitten pose? Or **Sophia Loren** pouring out of a sundress? I'd been in airport terminals before, but not one with hallways lined with paparazzi photos of goddesses snapped on the tarmac as they arrived in the South of France. I'd come to the Cannes Film Festival for exactly this kind of sexy, European-flavored glamour. A first-timer, I was primed to join the jet-setters' club. Pour me a kir royale, *cherie*, and keep them coming. But do I have to wear a sundress with these spindly legs?

The story of how I got to Cannes starts with a confession. When I was in junior college in the 1980s. **Joan Rivers** had a show on Fox, *The Late Show.* They did a publicity stunt where

Yo Mama? A mother and son reunion (at least in my delusional mind)
(Photo courtesy of the author)

they asked viewers to submit a videotape to get a chance to be on the show. I worshiped Joan Rivers. I thought she was hilarious and I admired how honest she was. I never saw her as mean-spirited, just an outlandish performer. I was hell-bent on winning this contest and becoming Joan's new best friend. I shot my tape at the Saidye Bronfman Centre after hours, with the help of one of the techies there. I came up with this idea that I was Joan Rivers's bastard son that she had tossed away on her way to the top, and I was going to blackmail her and tell the world the truth. So I did a cheap ripoff of Joan. I did a lot of

"Can we tawks?" and waved my death-metal long hair around. I sent it to her. A couple of months later a bright pink envelope arrived and on the corner, it said THE JOAN RIVERS SHOW.

I ripped open the envelope, and it was a letter from Joan saying, "I liked all the jokes about you being my illegitimate son." It was a warm letter signed by her. The letter also mentioned that if I was ever in L.A., I should come see the show and meet her afterward. I read between the lines and took this as an invitation: "Come live with me in Bel Air." After that, I really became obsessed with Joan Rivers. It was time to save every penny and make a quick trip to L.A. A few months later, I was ready to embark on my Become One With Joan journey. But first I needed to lose my heavy-metal hair—I was doing it for Joanie. I didn't want her to get scared, or to look at me and say, "What an ugly girl." I thought Joan would much prefer my new respectable 'do: a fluffy, feathered crop that made me look like a CPA. A few weeks before I went out to L. A., I called Joan Rivers's assistant. My voice shook as I said, "Ms. Rivers said to call if I was coming into town." And the secretary answered, "Absolutely. I understand." My ticket was to be waiting at Fox Studios.

I can't even remember who the guests were on the show. They could have been propped up corpses for all I cared. The whole time, I kept thinking about what would I say to my idol, and who would get first dibs on the bathroom once we lived together. After the show, an assistant came up to me and brought me to the stage where Joan was doing a meet-and-greet. She had various people there waiting to meet her, and I

THE LATE SHOW
STARRING

February 5, 1987

Dear Steven,

Thanks so much for your videotape.

This is just a quick note to let you know how much I personally appreciate the expenditure of your time and effort and talent.

I especially liked all the jokes about being my illegitimate son.

If you're ever in L.A. when we're broadcasting the show, please call my secretary, Jodee at (213) 555-5555 and she will arrange for you to view the show in the studio audience. Afterward, I would be delighted to meet you.

Thanks again for your interest. My personal friends kid me. They say that I seem like I love being a star. Truth is, I do. And one of the best parts of being a star is being flattered by talented and interested people like you. You've really made me very happy.

I hope to see you soon.

Best regards,

Joan Rivers

jr:vc407

learned a valuable lesson about hard work in show business: Joan Rivers was like a politician. She clocked in a fresh fan greeting and handshake every five minutes.

Edgar, Joan's husband, shuffled around tired, looking like he had the weight of the world on his shoulders. And there was Joan, looking much smaller than I had expected her to look. With her personality I thought she'd be the height of a linebacker, and not this underweight Chihuahua in spike heels and a tailored white blazer and sleek navy skirt. Then, my BIG moment happened. I had prepared my line for her for three months already. They said, "Joan, this is Steven." And I went, "Mother!" She broke down laughing.

Then there's a postscript to this, and a double postscript. I became a quasi-stalker to Joan because I decided, in my mind, that we were friends. I wrote her letters. I did drawings for her, vicious caricatures of Hollywood stars like the cartoon I did of Elizabeth Taylor's bosom exploding. She would write me letters back: "I loved your note. Loved your pictures." We became pen pals and, when Edgar passed away, I sent my condolences. She sent me back a thank-you note and told me she appreciated my kind words.

I can't say that I know the real, intimate Joan Rivers—even though she did one time say she wanted to sleep with me—but I do know one side of Joan Rivers. I know her to be a woman with manners, who is caring, and who gave some attention to a punk from Nowhere, Canada. Now that I have a career in this business, I see how time is the most precious thing. And Joan took the time out to respond to me. She made me feel like

I mattered.

My trip to Cannes was booked at the last minute. All the good hotels were full. When the travel agent suggested a nearby village, I thought, "How charming." But surely the cab driver had taken a wrong turn and made a left into downtown Bosnia. I was trapped in a shantytown—with dilapidated buildings left for dead during the war—buried in the mountains. And my lodgings, the ten-room inn with the—gulp—shared *toilette* was nothing more than a Motel 6 with a French accent.

My first morning, I decided to get in touch with my inner explorer and walk down the mountain to Cannes. Of course, a major butch voyager outfit was in order: I threw on a clingy see-through Dolce & Gabbana white tank top, white gauzy balloon drawstring pants and single-toe Yves Saint Laurent hippie sandals. But that didn't say seen-it-all navigator enough to *moi*. The ensemble begged for oversized Jackie O sunglasses and a white, straw cowboy hat as final touches. In my mind, it was very Marrakesh bedouin chic meets the Côte d'Azur. In reality, it was more like an outfit that would only play at a karaoke bar in Ibiza.

During the mid-1990s, *People*'s "Stylewatch" column just kept growing and growing. Carol Wallace, the editor of *People*, really liked that page and supported it. Carol took me under her wing and molded me into a strong reporter. I always tell her she took Pippi Longstocking and made her into a man. So I met every star in Hollywood for that column. Some people are speed

I didn't set out to look like a Dr. Seuss character for this Oscar-week party tossed by Tom Ford of Gucci. I realize now that I made a huge fashion faux pas—one should never wear a vintage goat cheveaux coat that blends with your highlights. Oops. *(© Jennifer Graylock)*

Mid-1980s. The toy poodle 'do that still haunts me. I have a recurring nightmare where I can't find my blow dryer and have to go out looking like this. *(Photo courtesy of the author)*

Late 1990s and adopting a Boho Abe Lincoln look! *(Photo courtesy of the author)*

Late 1980s—my last stab at looking respectable. I'm primed to enter a Jerry Seinfeld look-alike contest. *(Photo courtesy of the author)*

RIGHT: *Access Hollywood*, March 2002:
On a shoot, but looking like an escaped
animal from Sigfried and Roy's menagerie.
(© Jennifer Graylock)

ABOVE: The MTV Video Awards,
August 2002: I got it into my head
that I wanted to look like
something from a circus—kind of a
Mick Jagger version of a
ringmaster. *(© Wireimage.com)*

RIGHT: The MTV Video Awards,
September 2001: My version of
red-carpet casual—a vintage
marabou-feather coat thrown
over an outlandish custom-made
t-shirt. I'd call this look
"Liberace: The Dark Side."
(© Wireimage.com)

The poor man's Lenny Kravitz at Oscar de la Renta's fashion show in New York City. *(© Jennifer Graylock)*

My signature cheeky tee-and-coat look at a Hugo Boss party. *(© Dimitrios Kambouris/FWD)*

Twins? A madcap in the best sense of the word, kindred
spirit and designer Betsy Johnson and me at a fashion fête
in New York City. *(© Patrick McMullent/Getty Images)*

Working the red carpet at the My VH-1 Awards, December 2001. I thought then that my coat was rock-star wild, but now it looks to me like a giant bath mat that would fit beautifully in my mom's powder room. (© *Vince Bucci/Getty Images*)

Flanked by my two fave glamour girls—Debra Messing and Angie Harmon—at a party in New York City following the *Vogue* VH-1 Fashion Awards. That pained look on my face is me thinking "Next to these babes, I look like a malnourished Lhasa Apso!" I was right! *(© Mazur/Wireimage.com)*

They're real! Taking in the view of Angie's chest. *(© Mazur/Wireimage.com)*

The cast of *Charlie's Angels III?* *(© Mazur/Wireimage.com)*

Some mementos. . .
(Courtesy of the author)

RALPH LAUREN
SPRING 2001

WEDNESDAY
SEPTEMBER 20TH
10:00 AM
387 WEST BROADWAY

F   2   O

SECTION   ROW   SEAT

PLEASE PRESENT THIS CARD FOR ADMISSION

CELINE

Steven Cojocaru

Collection Printemps-Eté 2001
Salle Le Nôtre
99, rue de Rivoli – Paris 1ᵉ
Mardi 10 Octobre 2000, à 19 heures précises

Secteur : **H**

Rang : **C15** 5

MISSONI
IS PLEASED TO INVITE

Steven Cojocaru

SUMMER 2001 COLLECTION
TUESDAY - OCTOBER 3 - 12:00 PM
FIERA DI MILANO
PIAZZA VI FEBBRAIO
SALA B

NEW LINE
CINEMA
INVITES YOU AND A GUEST
TO JOIN THE CAST AND FILMMAKERS
AT THE WORLD PREMIERE OF

AUSTIN
POWERS
International Man Of Mystery

MONDAY, APRIL 28, 1997
7:30 P.M.
MANN'S CHINESE THEATRE
6925 HOLLYWOOD BOULEVARD
HOLLYWOOD

PARTY IMMEDIATELY FOLLOWING AT
THE HOLLYWOOD COLONNADE
6840 HOLLYWOOD BOULEVARD
HOLLYWOOD

HOTEL
PRINCIPE DI SAVOIA
Milano

BAGAGLIO
Luggage

Camera N.

223
3P.

N° 2847

TOMMY ■ HILFIGER
SPRING 2000 MEN'S AND WOMEN'S COLLECTION
Tuesday, September 14   8:00 PM
The Theater at Madison Square Garden
Entrance on 8th Avenue and 31st Street

demons. I was a star demon. From your Julias to your Toms—I interviewed everybody. And I was, all too often, disappointed. Very quickly, I tuned in to their flaws and foibles. When you're talking to a movie legend at the Oscars and she's got painted-on eyebrows and mounds of "Hello Bella Lugosi" makeup on, it kind of takes the mystique away.

But television just kept calling me. I went to countless auditions. Once I tried out to be a VJ on MTV. In my mind, to be a VJ on MTV was to be very colorful. So I poured myself into a pair of skintight Moschino jeans with Mona Lisa's face silk-screened all over them. The calendar said 1995, but my taste was still trapped in the '80s. I wore—I'm embarrassed to say—a leather vest with no shirt underneath. And biker boots. And that horrible Steven Segal rip-off ponytail. Suffice it to say, I did not get the gig.

My big break came when Elycia Rubin, the fashion director at E!, saw something beyond the ponytail. Elycia has become one of my great friends—she's a major glamour girl and a striking brunette with emerald eyes. She started offering me spots on *E! News Daily* and E! specials. Eventually she invited me onto the one-hour "Oscar Fashion Review" with Joan Rivers and her daughter Melissa. This was an opportunity, but I was terrified—I would be up close and personal with Joan. Would she remember her gushing Montreal fanboy?

The Oscars were on a Monday. On Tuesday morning we had a seven-thirty A.M. production meeting at E! The guests on the show were designer Carolina Herrera, myself, and Frederic Fekkai, the celebrity hairdresser. Frederic sailed in with freshly

77

HOW TO FISH FOR DISH AT A HOLLYWOOD PARTY

Keep Moving: Schmoozing is a numbers game, so abide by the thirty-second rule: Never talk to the same person for more than thirty seconds (unless it's Brad, Julia, George, or a plastic surgeon offering a free consultation). Use a stopwatch if you have to.

Ignore Rule #1 Occasionally and Park Yourself at the Bar: Everybody drinks something. Keep your notepad handy—if there's one rule in Hollywood, it's that Russell Crowe will always end up at the bar.

Send a Girl to the Bathroom: Alas, I can't go myself—but I'll send a trained substitute. There's nothing like a communal lipgloss application to get a star talking about her tummy tuck. This does not hold true for the men's room. Most male celebrities are pee-shy. You'd be, too, if you had a bulky, motorized penis pump to work around.

washed, tousled hair that artfully fell in the right places around his face. He was immaculately turned out in a sharp blazer, a painstakingly pressed shirt and slacks, and gleaming loafers. I detested him on sight. But he was so incredibly charming, I came around and we've since remained friendly. Though I'll never be able to get my locks to tousle so obediently.

Then there was the ultimate class act, Carolina Herrera. So stylish, so composed. She mesmerized me. I was happy to just gawk at her from afar, but then spoke to me. And it turned out that this great elegant lady was full of life and mischievious humor. This was a revelation: I didn't think wearing silk georgette and being earthy went together. After that I felt perfectly comfortable grilling Carolina about her fabled friends: "You knew Jackie O," I sighed. "Do you have a used towel she owned? I'd like to put it under plexiglass in my living room."

"With all that collagen, I had to wear a lobster bib to avoid being splattered on."

Then it was time for Joan's grand entrance. She didn't have a stitch of makeup on. I'll hold back on describing the sight except to say that to this day I still experience grizzly flashbacks of the image, probably not that dissimilar to the post-trauma Desert Storm soldiers suffer from. But the early-morning outfit was killer. Joan took her seat at the head of the board room table wrapped in a cashmere coat with a gigantic fox-fur collar. Joan Crawford would probably have made the same choice. I was wildly intimidated. Joan looked at me and boomed, "How were the Oscars last night?" I blurted out, "With all that collagen, I had to wear a lobster bib to avoid being splattered on."

She just lost it. She looked at me and said, "I like you!" She sounded like Harvey Fierstein. She didn't remember that I was the delusional fan who claimed to be her son. I've never brought it up in all the time we've known each other; I've been too embarrassed. Right off the bat I saw that Joan was about the work. We were plotting out the show and she said, "Okay, we're going to get to this part of the show, Steven, and you're going to do this." I started throwing out some jokes, and she went, "I like that! I like that! Put that joke in. Yeah! Do that!" The one thing I can tell you about Joan Rivers is that there's not one lazy bone in this woman's body.

Then came the crash course. I got to see how long Joan spent in makeup (three days with naps during the sand blasting). She and Melissa each had her own hair and makeup person. A lightbulb went off for me. I thought, "Oh, so that's how it's done. You get professionals to put you together." Choosing clothes for the show was half the battle. I put on a burgundy crushed-velvet designer jacket by Krizia, the high-end Italian clothing line. I wore this blazer with leather pants, platforms, spiky hair, and a goatee. I was weird looking. I was certainly no Frederic Fekkai.

Suddenly, we were On Air and I was getting where Joan was coming from. What we were talking about—Oscar night fashion—was so silly and insubstantial, playfully mocking it seemed appropriate. It was all so natural that it was frightening. I sat there with Joan and Melissa and I didn't see myself as any big expert. I was just giving my honest opinion and not holding back.

But I didn't realize the power of television. This was the year that **Jennifer Lopez** came to the Oscars in a black satin strapless Badgley Mischka gown with a big poofy skirt. She had very light makeup and her hair pulled back into a bun—she looked like a Hollywood princess. But a few months before she had been looking really trashy. So on the special Joan asked, "What do you think of Jennifer Lopez?" And I said, "She's definitely most improved. She was one of my favorite dressers. She went from slut to princess in one fell swoop."

This was the probably the first of fifty times that I've jokingly called Jennifer Lopez a slut on television. I say that with tongue firmly in cheek because I do admire Jennifer Lopez. In my book, she's interesting, and interesting will always win over bland. But she's also a target. Sometimes with J. Lo., she looks like an over-the-top, tarty wild, pop-star street girl. Other times she gives you Audrey Hepburn. She plays both roles very well.

Because it was one of my first times on TV, I felt really bad. I was scared. She was dating **Puffy** then. I went home and told my friends, "Oh my God, I called Jennifer Lopez a slut on television and Puffy is going to come after me. He's going to tie me to a chair and bitch-slap me." I got paranoid. I pulled the blinds down. Every time a twig hit my window, I dived under the bed. I wore a bulletproof Laura Ashley pajama set to bed that week. But no one said a word. I think it was a rite of passage for me: Once I said the word *slut* on television, I have never looked back. I never censored myself again.

It was pretty heady to be on television in a town where people watch the Oscar coverage that closely. People really noticed me. Strangers started talking to me. Tables started getting better at restaurants. Instead of keeping me waiting an hour and a half, my hairdresser Byron would only keep me waiting thirty minutes.

The best-kept secret in Hollywood is that your stock in

Jennifer Lopez in Hollywood Princess mode at the Oscars
(©Mark Stephenson/CORBIS)

Hollywood really has nothing to do with box office or the freebies you get or the invitations you get. It has everything to do with waiting time. The bigger you are the less you wait.

A couple of months later a wondrous thing happened. Elycia called me from E! and asked me to go to Cannes to do Joan Rivers's Cannes fashion review show. That was unreal. I was like, "What? Say that again? Can you repeat that? You're asking me to go to Cannes and appear with Joan Rivers?" You had to scrape me off the floor.

There's more hysteria at Cannes than there is at the Oscars—and Joan, Melissa, and I were in the middle of it. We were shooting the special right on the main drag, the Croisette. It gave us a great view of the main population of Cannes during the film festival—goons and bimbos. Both factions were hard at work. Every few feet, there's an ape working security. The French might be wonderful at transforming bread and cheese into culinary brilliance, but they're not so adept at hiring security personnel. One minute you're a guy named Henri hanging on the beach in a microscopic thong and the next someone throws a few francs at you and you're patrolling the Croisette. Cannes is also home to the biggest breast implants on Earth—massive-chested women with breasts the size of a helipad doing anything to get photographed.

The best-kept secret in Hollywood is that your stock in Hollywood really has nothing to do with box office or the freebies you get or the invitations you get. It has everything to do with waiting time. The bigger you are the less you wait.

We just went to town on everybody at Cannes. I felt really feisty and so did Joan. This older French couple was walking on the dock, completely oblivious to the fact that we were in the middle of taping. They were walking to the dinghy that would take them to their yacht. Did I mention they were trashy? This woman was definitely in her fifties or sixties and she was wearing—barely—a gold-lamé bikini and cha-cha high heels. Her husband, weighed down by a ton of jewelry, looked like a troll dipped in gold. I eyed Joan and whispered, "Ugh, Joan. Look at that Eurotrash couple." And Joan started yelling at them, screaming at the top of her lungs, "Eurotrash! Euro-trash!"

We shot for most of the morning, and then we had to take a two-hour break. Perfect opportunity, I thought, to go back to my room and pack the towels that I had to steal for my mother. Towel burglary is big in my family. If there were an inordinate amount of towels missing from the Marco Polo Hotel in Miami Beach in the 1970s, they were lifted by my mother. My mother was and is a consummate towel, ashtray, and soap collector. You've been warned.

I was about to leave, but Joan stopped me. "Absolutely not! We're going back to my hotel room," she declared. "We're going to order room service and I want to get to know you." From my dump to her no-doubt swanky digs would have been a relief. Except I wasn't the only one with hotel woes. I responded, "I guess we're going to your suite at the Majestic where there's a grand piano in the bathroom." And she said, "Not quite. I'm on an E! budget. I'm staying in a shitty rathole of a hotel room on the outskirts of Cannes."

Off we went to Joan's hotel and it certainly was no Ritz. But we kicked off our shoes and got into bed.

It was a Steven Cojocaru sandwich, with Melissa on one side and Joan on the other. We ordered sandwiches and gabbed for two hours. All that was missing was a bowl of popcorn and a video of *Steel Magnolias*. What really impressed me was that Joan wanted to hear about me—most stars are unable to see past their own altered noses.

I was working nonstop at Cannes, and at one point I was fried. I slipped away for an hour to catch my breath and dip my foot in the water. Across the street from all the top hotels, there are docks with little dinghies that deliver the hoi-polloi to the big yachts. I snuck onto the dock of the *It was a Steven Cojocaru sandwich* chichi Majestic Hotel—the grande dame of Cannes hotels—and plopped myself on a chaise lounge. I was staring into space when I happened to look up, and there was **Jerry Hall**, all legs, wearing a sarong, a one-piece bathing suit, stilettos, and a gigantic straw hat. She looked glam and trashy at the same time. This was after she had broken up with Mick Jagger, and it was very fresh in the headlines. She wasn't looking too traumatized. Newly single Jerry was about to be picked up in a dinghy and whisked off to a monster yacht in the horizon.

That evening, I covered the AmFAR benefit (for the American Foundation for AIDS Research). It's one of the biggest parties at Cannes: **Liz Hurley**, **Elton John**, **Elizabeth Taylor**, **Salma Hayek**, **Ben Affleck**, and **Jerry Hall** were there. I approached

The dock at the Majestic Hotel in Cannes, all spiffy and ready for Jerry Hall's arrival

Ben Affleck, but I was apprehensive. The last time I had spoken to him was on the red carpet at the Oscars and he was a surly jerk. I had asked the numbingly fluffy question, "So what did you do today?" Fluff apparently didn't agree with him. "I whacked off in the shower," he hissed. We clearly had nowhere to go from there so I said, "Thank you. Good-bye." (Fortunately, **Matt Damon** was right behind him and I told Matt exactly what Ben had said. His whole face lit up and he laughed. He gave me that million-dollar close-up that studios have to pay for and said, "Did he really say that? Shame on him!" Matt good cop, Ben bad cop.)

But here, in the perfect evening light of Cannes, Affleck was incredibly gracious and very, very Chatty Cathy. Dare I say, down-to-earth? Basically, stars can be so moody.

Above: Chatty Cathy Ben in Cannes *(©AFP/CORBIS). Right:* Liz Hurley in Cannes. How do you say T&A–fest in French? *(©Reuters NewMedia Inc./CORBIS)*

Speaking of which: **La Liz** swung by and stopped by our table. We've all seen Liz Taylor with her ups and downs—this was Liz in a not-particularly-good moment. It looked like someone had spliced together five caftans for her to wear. When she saw Melissa Rivers, she shrieked with delight. She said, "Melissa, darling. How are you? How's your mother? Tell her hello."

It's interesting to be around children of Hollywood like Melissa, because they've seen it all and done it all. As soon as Liz was dragged away, Melissa was so cynical. She shrugged and said, "Sometimes I see her, she's warm and nice. Too nice, really. Other times, she's not. We just got a good night." I was

All that was missing was a copy of *Steel Magnolias* when I spent the afternoon in bed with Joan and Melissa in a fleabag hotel in Cannes. *(©Reuters NewMedia Inc./CORBIS)*

with Melissa when she later told Joan about the Liz moment. "Ugh. She's back on the sauce," zinged Joan. That was so Joan—a nice tidy comment to size up the situation.

Since Cannes, Joan Rivers has done some incredibly nice things for me. She sent my mom some Joan Rivers jewelry and a note saying, "I'm crazy about your son. You brought him up well." That made my mother weep.

We see each other a lot on the plane back and forth to New York. She'll scoot onto the plane in full makeup, perfect hair, a gorgeous black Hermés bag, and a black wool wrap with a mink collar. She has phenomenal legs—she's the white Tina Turner. She'll slink into the free seat beside me and say, "Lucky you." And I answer, "No, no, honey. Lucky you."

One time, on the plane with Joan, we were sitting next to the NBC lawyer for the *Today Show.* She came up to me and said, "Oh, we're working on your contract right now." So Joan started negotiating my contract. She was joking, but she was hilarious. She said, "Whatever he asked for, we want double now." Another time, we gossiped for five and a half hours. This was a red-eye to New York, and somewhere over Milwaukee, at four in the morning, we concocted a list of who had the worst plastic surgery in Hollywood. (Joan didn't volunteer her name, and I didn't push it.) The number-one person on our list was the fortysomething blond actress married to a hunk movie star. Just think fiberglass lips, a contorted face, and eyes tucked back to the point where you almost think she's a Korean flight attendant. Our lips are sealed.

SIX

THE GOATEE
OR MATT LAUER?

The bridesmaid of Frankenstein—me before my mandatory
Today Show makeover. *(©Jennifer Graylock)*

There are some things that I will lay my body down to defend—I always thought my goatee was one of them.

In the late 1990s, I had grown what is know in hipster parlance as a soul patch (a patch of hair hugging the chin) with the idea that if you can't be good-looking, then at least look interesting. But I still felt like an exclamation point was missing. So I got my soul-patch its very own hair-extension. I glued it under my chin and then I took black M.A.C. mascara and painted my fu-manchu chin-piece jet black to go with my jet-black hair and penciled black eyebrows.

I was going for a vampire look. Except I was the one who got bit on the derriere. At the MTV Movie Awards in Santa Monica, I was backstage and I bumped into **Cameron Diaz**. We've bumped into each other every so often over the years and it's schmoozey-schmoozey friendly between us. But that night, I had gone pretty wild with the mascara on the goatee. Nothing was black enough. When I said good-bye to Cameron,

Steven Cojocaru

I gave her a little European kiss on both cheeks. About ten minutes later, I passed by her in the Green Room. She had black smudges from my mascara on her face—wimpy me didn't tell her. Me and my leaking half-goatee ran away instead.

This freaky, black half-goatee became my signature style. As sinister as I might have looked, I got noticed. In the summer of 2000, a few months after *People*'s PR director Susan Ollinick brought me to meet Betsy Alexander, a top producer at *Today*, Betsy called about my availability. "We like that kooky guy who works for you. We want to get into business with him," she said. "But he needs a makeover, or he'll scare people in the morning. The goatee has to go."

No goatee or no job. I was "too scary" for morning television. My reaction was, "I'm an artist. How dare you try and interfere with my artistic expression? This is censorship!" Besides, who wants to be "morning-friendly" anyway? But Ollinick, who is really blunt, said to me in the nicest way, "Forget artistic expression. It's the *Today* show. You're shaving off the goatee. End of story." She gave me a deadline: three weeks.

The truth was, I still felt extremely unattractive, and the goatee protected me. It was my armor. If we all have any demon that we fight with, mine was the demon of feeling unattractive. And after being a teenager with untamable frizzy hair and buck teeth—I was scared to see myself without any shield.

I shaved it all off at once. There was so much gel and mascara in it, it sort of snapped off. And it was like the sun had come up. I looked at myself in the mirror and said, "This face isn't so bad." It was the beginning of a healing and acceptance. Without expecting it, I was finally getting comfortable in my own skin. To this day I kiss Betsy's feet because she looked beyond my **Marilyn Manson** façade and saw the person who didn't bite.

Since they were expanding to a third hour, the *Today* show wanted to come out blazing. They wanted to send me to Milan and Paris for two weeks to report live from the ready-to-wear fashion shows. This was my audition.

I was completely jumping out of my skin. For my first assignment, I was going to biggest fashion event of the year. Armani, Versace, Prada, and Courtney Love in the house.

I went to Milan first. I got paired up with an amazing producer, Jackie Olensky, and we were like two nice Jewish girls in Europe watching over each other's chastity and encouraging each other to spend a lot of money shopping. We absolutely bonded—in part because I was tickled that her nickname was Jackie O.

There are two hotels for any of the fashionista out-of-towners in Milan for the fashion shows: the Four Seasons, considered civilized and chic, and the Principe de Savoya, which is a gaudy explosion. Guess which one I picked. All the models stay at the Principe de Savoya, and after a day of shows, all the fashionistas get sloshed in the lobby bar. I wasn't the only one who preferred a hotel whose main draw was drunken models tripping through the halls. **George Clooney**, **Leonardo DiCaprio** and **Courtney Love** were also counting sheep under the same roof.

Courtney and I keep crossing paths. She is one of my favorite celebrities because she doesn't play it safe. So many celebrities are so careful and artificial. Courtney Love is an unbridled bad girl and I enjoy catching her high-wire act. There's "angry" Courtney, in the lobby of the Sunset 5 movie theater in L.A. When I put my tape recorder too close to her for a quote, she screamed "Get that fucking tape recorder out of my face or I'm going to make you eat it!" There's "nice" Courtney, walking down Bedford Drive where I'm coming out of Anastasia Salon after having my unibrow attended to. She looks like a schoolgirl in a spiffy cashmere sweater set and capri pants. She calls out, "Hey fashion dude!" and waves sweetly. Then there's "paranoid" Courtney, at the BMG post-Grammys party, where she is completely incoherent and whispering to me that some German guy is following her. When she saw Howard Stern, she dropped me like I was a call-waiting beep that she wasn't interested in.

But my favorite moment with Courtney was in the lobby of the Principe. She sweeps in with her little girl, Frances Bean, and she doesn't have a stitch of makeup on. We have a big reunion in the lobby like I'm her long-lost Siamese mutant twin. We take the elevator together. And although she's au naturel, I'm flabbergasted: she's beautiful. And I told her. For somebody with so much bravado, she blushed. She introduced me to her daughter. Frances already looked like a mini-me Courtney. She was wearing a leather Versace dress. Even though Courtney is painted as a fellow freak like me, I found little Frances to be so well-mannered. She shook my hand, looked me square in the

Didn't you know that blondes like Donatella and Courtney grow on trees in Milan? *(©Corbis)*

eye. Bet she could already stir a mean martini and rattle off the names of the top sushi restaurants in New York City.

Time to get to work: I spent most days squeezed inside a minivan with Jackie and the crew. I always got stuck sitting in the front seat with our driver, who was so heavy I was sure he was being fed pasta primavera intravenously. But he had the soul of a race-car driver, almost breaking the sound barrier flying through the tiny streets of Milan. We went first to the packed opening of the frightfully chic Giorgio Armani superstore, a block-long department store housing everything Armani. Even the escalator, stairs, and doorknobs were designer-perfect.

Mr. Armani would be my first interview. He's an intimidating presence from the get-go. He's got the most gorgeous snow-white hair I've ever seen. He's quite handsome too, with the piercing blue eyes and a perfect Mediterranean tan. He's known to be deadly serious so I try to collect myself. We had to talk through a translator, but I guess my vapid language is international because I jumped right into the most pressing question on my mind: "You are such a perfectionist, do you ever do anything wrong? Have you ever overcooked pasta?" And that made him giggle. Later that day, we went to the Armani fashion show and **Robert DeNiro** and **Sophia Loren** were there. Sophia gave me 'tude. I met her at the Oscars and she was so lovely, I expected her to remember me and invite me over for a veal scalloppini dinner. But she was chilly and told me she didn't want to be interviewed. I said, "Miss Loren, I want to talk to you about Giorgio Armani. He's your friend. You're breaking my heart and his." She laughed, and I got my interview (but no veal scalloppini).

The Armani show was extraordinary. The clothes, the models, the music—it was all so beautifully executed. It was held in an amphitheater in Armani's sprawling house. Since we were there to interview people, I worked the front row, which is reserved primarily for celebrities, since that's who the cameras will catch. I would go up to stars and ask them frothy questions. It's a very strained situation because you're crouching down and shoving a microphone in someone's face. Forget about looking dignified.

George and Sophia at Armani are all smiles, but I'm crouching beneath them begging for a soundbite. *(©Reuters NewMedia Inc./CORBIS)*

It was time for me to go on-air with a Milan wrap-up report. I'd be on live and then we'd throw to the footage we had been shooting at the shows all week. Of course, I had spent the day before obsessing over the perfect *Today* show debut outfit. What about that Gaultier black leather jacket with the chain detail? Maybe a little too S & M for the morning? In the end, I thought wearing an elegant Italian label would be fitting. I called Gucci about borrowing an ensemble. They invited me up to their showroom. It felt like a Gidget Goes to Milan moment when I excitedly walked into Gucci's sleek, mirrored Milan headquarters. They brought out this stunning dark-orange leather motorcycle jacket for me—I matched it with tan motorcycle pants and dark brown Gucci biker boots. I would have gargled with Gucci mouthwash if they had any.

Jackie and the crew went to the location ahead of me to set up. We were going to beam from smack-dab in the center of a busy town square. When I arrived there I saw a huge satellite truck and lots of technical hardware. Yikes, this looked like the kind of big-league TV setup they would have for Tom Brokaw reporting from a political summit. The butterflies in my stomach were beginning to do backflips. Jackie put me in position and told me Katie and Matt would come to me any minute. Instead, a flock of birds decided to visit first. It seemed like there were hundreds of vultures circling just above my head: No, shoo, scram! I was gripped by the fear that Gucci had a "If birds defecate on it, you buy it" policy.

Jackie signaled that New York was coming to me for a quick teaser. "*People* magazine's West Coast style editor Steven Cojocaru is in Milan for us," Katie said. "Good morning, Steven, I love that jacket—is that for spring?" "Actually, Katie, this jacket is so far ahead it's from the winter 2005 collection," I tossed out. Matt and Katie got me immediately and laughed. They were generous and affable to the absolute extreme. They made me look good. An hour later, we came back and I did the whole report on Milan Fashion Week. I talked about Gisele the supermodel and I promised to bring her back to Matt as a present. I said, "Do you want socks or Gisele?" He turned beet-red. I rather enjoyed that, I must admit.

Afterward, Jackie and I went out to celebrate. We went shopping on the Via Monte Napaloni and something really wonderful came into my life. It's a word that I often say to myself to get calm and centered: "Discount." The PR person at Gucci was very lovely and said all the editors who come from the States can walk into their store and show their cards to get discounts. There's a list that they cross-check and I made it. We went shopping at Gucci, and then to Prada, and I just kept whipping out my card. I bought a Prada fur hat that three seasons later came into vogue. It was such a big splurge. I foolishly spent a thousand dollars on a hat, something I wouldn't do today. Real estate is a far more soothing accessory.

The jet-setter wannabe in me thoroughly enjoyed winging from Milan to Paris. It was continental; so Brigitte meets Sophia. I called all my friends from the Milan airport to say, "Hi, What are you doing today? Oh, you're gardening or getting your car washed? I'm flying from Milan to Paris."

I stayed at the chic Plaza Athénée in Paris, largely because that's where Jackie O (Onassis, not Olensky) and Ari used to frolic. I thought if I was going to communicate with Jackie's spirit, this was the place to do it. So in the middle of the night, in my petite room with the pale-yellow walls, I tried giving her a shout-out: "Jackie, can you hear me?" Apparently her afterlife cell phone was off. Nevertheless, I called my mother to gleefully tell her I was at the Plaza Athénée just like Jackie had been—Mom knew it from all the books she had read about Jackie. She was happy to be living vicariously through my own vicarious shenanigans.

First stop in Paris was the Valentino show, held in a grand hall at the Louvre. Valentino's setting was typical of most of the top designer spectacles in Paris. A powerful backdrop steeped in history is the only civilized way to go. The French really know how to give good show.

As any fashion reporter worth his Cavalli leather biker jacket knows, you always get to a fashion show early to scope out who is sitting where. Most of the time the seats have a sheet of paper with the guest's name on it. At the Valentino show, Hugh Grant was right beside the princess of Bulgaria. I met up with Hugh backstage—he was being very bratty. The paparazzi were waiting by his seat to photograph him, but I heard him whine that he didn't want to face the fray until seconds before the show was to start. Or maybe he didn't want to give up his unobstructed view of all the half-naked models. Valentino, meanwhile, was so elegant. Even his eyelashes were groomed.

It was time to get outfitted for my segment from Paris. I had done one report on the *Today* show and Mr. Rebel was already itching to break the "morning friendly" image rule. This time, I would truly be me. I picked out a severe-looking black crinkled patent-leather coat, a black cashmere sweater, and black leather pants from the Italian fashion house Costume National. Wearing high-end designer clothes—even loaner garb that has a twenty-four-hour expiration date until the fashion marshals come looking for them—was so new to me, I actually laid the clothes on my bed and caressed them. To this day, every time I return a get-up to a designer, I have a fear it will be the last fabulous outfit I'll be loaned. Some people have nightmares about falling off cliffs; I have nightmares that I'll be forced to go the Oscars in my gray-sweater-and-cords college uniform.

With the outfit squared away, it was time to turn my attention to a matter of such grave importance I'm surprised it didn't make the front page of *Le Monde*: STEVEN ON HUNT FOR HAIR-DRESSER. But not just any hairdresser, it had to be *the* stylist of Paris. I asked around and kept getting the same response: "Oh, no one should touch your hair except Thierry." It seemed that Thierry only had one name because that's all he needed. He was, everyone kept telling me, the hair artiste who tended to Naomi Campbell's 'do whenever she flitted through Paris. But getting Thierry anywhere near your unknown follicles is no easy feat. You basically had to apply, much like the agonizing process one goes through to get into an Upper East Side co-op. But I had a friend who knew a friend who was acquainted with someone who occasionally slept with the hair guru. I was in.

Thierry and his multiple piercings arrived at the Plaza Athénée fresh from coiffing the models at the Chanel show. He gave me the once-over and seemed less than impressed. "What do you want me to do?" he huffed. I told him to give me a rock-star look. He rolled his eyes and seemed to block me out. But a hair-obsessed fashionista wasn't going to take Thierry's apathetic flat-ironing lying down. This was going to be a joint architectural project. "No, Thierry, this is the way the bangs go. This is the exact ninety-degree angle that this hair has to flip up on this side. And this side has to bend: not curl, but bend. And this piece here goes over my eye in a sultry Veronica Lake meets Steven Tyler kind of feeling." He was perspiring the entire time. When Thierry finished, he collapsed into a chair and said, "Mon dieu! You are more difficult than Naomi!"

Those were fighting words. There's no greater insult in my world than having a hairdresser tell you you're more high maintenance than the notorious high priestess of high mainte-nance Naomi Campbell. I wanted to stick Thierry's round brush on a piece of baguette bread and force-feed it to him. In-stead, I put the slam to end all slams to productive use. When I got on the air with my Paris report on *Today*, the first thing I said was, "I'm devastated. Naomi Campbell's hairdresser did my hair and said I was more high maintence than Naomi." There's nothing like a little on-air therapy.

Everything felt natural with my second *Today* segment. Katie saw me on the monitor and said I looked like Prince—I could have saved NBC the money on airfare and floated back home. I did my dispatch. The big spring fashions that year were very masculine, hard-edged fashions for women. Near the end of the segment, Matt asked me, "Did you see anything feminine?"

I retorted, "Only the guys backstage."

As soon as I got off the air, Jeff Zucker, then the executive producer of the *Today* show and now the president of NBC En-tertainment, called Jackie on her cell phone. The verdict was in. "This guy's a keeper," he said. "I want him in-studio next week."

SEVEN

CHARLIZE THE GLAMAZON VERSUS GWYNETH THE MCNUGGET

The 56th Annual Golden Globe Awards Presentation

International Ballroom
Beverly Hilton Hotel
Sunday, January 24, 1999

Black Tie

- 2:30 PM Cocktails
- 3:30 PM Champagne Supper
- 5:00 PM Awards Presentation Live on NBC

Price $ 500.00

DOORS CLOSE AT 4:45

Name STEVEN COJOCARU (Pres)

Table No. 313

No 1164

(Absolutely No Cameras or Tape Recorders Permitted)

Columbia TriStar Motion
56th Annual Golden Globe
Immediately Following the Awa

Sunday, January 24

Beverly Hilton Ho
"Under the Stars on the Ro
9876 Wilshire Boulevar
Beverly Hills

Please take the guest elevators in the main lobby

ADMIT ONE

"*G* *lamour Boy." There's no exact Webster's definition for it. I won't argue that the term certainly conjures up an image of a superficial party-hopper. Who, me? Let's make that a working glamour boy instead. Need proof? Help yourself to my Palm Pilot and see what the four seasons of a professional gadfly look like . . .*

January:
Red Carpet, Golden Globes

I'm swathed in a floor-length black mink coat—because I'm allergic to tuxedos and I was going through a P. Diddy moment. The red carpet scene is basically over. But nobody told Charlize Theron that.

I'm taping my wrap-up fashion reviews with Shawn Robinson for *Access Hollywood* on a desolate red carpet. All of a sudden, **Charlize Theron** appears. She's really late and flying

Better late than never: Charlize Theron at the Golden
Globes minutes before our "engagement"
(©Reuters NewMedia Inc./CORBIS)

solo. She's really sexed out in a black Christina Perrin gown with big cutouts showing off ample cleavage and midriff. Lots of stars look good in pictures but in person—without their on-call airbrushers—they're nothing to write home about. Charlize is take-your-breath-away beautiful in person. And frighteningly statuesque. In heels she's about seven foot three. Waify Gwyneth is a McNugget next to her.

I just start to mess with her. "Why are you so late?" I ask, with the cameras on. But she doesn't take the bait. So I fling myself at her feet and go, "You're so beautiful it's painful." I start bowing—I've never bowed in front of anybody on the red carpet before, but I do it for her. I say, "I'm madly in love with you." It just pops out. Then she says, "I'm madly in love with you," and grabs me. "You're my date tonight," she proclaims, dragging me down the carpet. A nauseatingly kiss-ass moment? You bet. But some people will do anything—including losing their dignity on the red carpet—to get something good for the camera. Luckily, good sport Charlize played along.

Charlize hasn't forgotten this. Over the summer, I bump into her at a Tom Ford party in Paris, for his new fragrance for Yves Saint Laurent called Nu. She's really wired, on the dance floor for a long time. I catch up with her at the bar and I say, "You haven't forgotten?" She swipes the sweat from her immaculate brow, lets every spotlight in the place find her, and says, "Of course I haven't forgotten. You're my fiancé."

February:
Mr. Chow, New York

Where did this crowd come from? It's like it's the heyday of Mr. Chow, back in the 1980s, when Andy Warhol and his hangers-on used to pack the place. I'm there for **Cynthia Garrett's** birthday party—Cynthia is a media personality who used to host NBC's *Later.*

Lenny Kravitz walks in with this babe on his arm who looks like he picked her off a Greyhound bus at Port Authority. She's maybe eighteen, nineteen—Lenny has a reputation for young girlfriends. She's wide-eyed like Cinderella. One minute she's nothing, the next she's canoodling with Lenny Kravitz.

I just launch into Lenny about how I would kill for his castoffs. All of a sudden we're talking about rock fashion and Lenny completely opens up. We end up sounding like two housewives talking about the new linen collection at Bloomingdale's. We yap about Cavalli vs. Gucci vs. Versace. I laugh and say, "Lenny, we have a lot in common. We're two nice Jewish boys who like to wear skintight leather pants."

At the end of the meal we all go to contribute, but Cynthia says, "Oh honey, you don't know the rule. When Lenny is out, Lenny picks up the bill. He gets insulted if anybody even dares put down money." I'm amazed—most celebrities are take, take, take, gimme, gimme, gimme. But Lenny picks up the tab for a dinner of thirty people.

February:

Wiltern Theater, Breathe Benefit for Breast Cancer

I have bleached blond–streaked hair, I'm decked out in leather head-to-toe, and I'm weighed down with tons of gold jewelry. I look like an extra in ghetto-fabulous video. Backstage is the company picnic of show business. This is really where you get to talk to people. The red carpet is artificial and forced by comparison. You get sound bites and you want stars to say clever things for the camera. Backstage is where you feel like you belong.

"You're a clone of Steven Tyler!" **Tom Hanks** announces. He's come back with his wife, **Rita Wilson**. He starts singing a medley of Aerosmith songs. Then we have an "I love you, man" moment. He slaps me on the back and says, "Steven, I'm so proud of what you've done with your career. Only in America could you come here, be this little reporter for *People* magazine, and now you're a style arbiter!" This is meaningful to me because Tom and Rita really watched me grow over the years. They were nice to me when I was this little tick from *People* magazine and was just beginning.

March:

South Beach, Miami

I need to rest up before the Oscars. So I flee to the Shore Club, one of the trendy hotels in Miami, hoping to chill out. Now, it's not really possible to hide out in South Beach. The last

Wherever I go, there's P. Diddy, the master schmoozer and the ultimate Good Time Charlie. *(Photo courtesy of the author)*

time I was in Miami, I couldn't escape **P. Diddy**. I was at a fête the La Prairie beauty products company threw for socialite Cornelia Guest at the Delano Hotel. When P. Diddy strolled in, Cornelia whispered to me that he wasn't on the party guest list. P. Diddy is one of the master schmoozers. He lives like he's one of the Rat Pack. I've seen him play DJ at parties and take off his shirt so that people will dance. At the Delano party, I busted him: "You're a party crasher." He grinned slyly and said, "I know I'm not on the list, but I just wanted to be close to you all." The next night, at a trendy club called Opium, he sent me a complimentary bottle of Cristal to make up for his peccadillo. There are not a lot of true *bons vivants* out there, but P. Diddy is one.

The weekend I'm in Miami turns out to be celebrity cluster. They're all at the Shore Club: **Whitney** and **Bobby** are holed up in a bungalow. **Wesley Snipes** is in his room doing jujitsu. **Lisa Ling**, **Heidi Klum**, and **Kyle MacLachlan** and myself plan to hook up for drinks—okay, I've scratched the whole "hiding out" idea—and who does Kyle bring along? His golfing buddy **Hugh Grant.**

We collected at a club called Mynt. It's amazing to see what a movie star with a playboy reputation is like. Women are throwing themselves at Hugh in the most obvious ways, and he juggles the harem expertly. They're writing their phone numbers on his arm. They're buying *him* drinks. He's loving every minute. I'm so turned off by hanging out with this horny toad and seeing the display that I become very anti-Hugh. To me he's like a rash.

I break off from the group with my friend Alice and we walk back to the hotel. An hour later we arrive at the foyer, and who do we bump into but poor wayward Hugh! It's two o'clock in the morning and he's with a male buddy—no female companionship. Something has clearly gone wrong. At this point Hugh looks like he's knocked back a few. All of a sudden

THE FASHIONISTA'S SURVIVAL PROGRAM

Evian Spray Bottle: Everybody in the fashion business in France walks around with this little atomizer of Evian water and you spray it on your face. It gives you this J. Lo-esque glow— dewy and fresh. I use it everywhere. People think it's mace.

Expensive Hair: Two words: *designer conditioner.* Mine has okra in it and I'm very heartened by that. I always know, if I'm close to a food coma, I can eat my hair.

Expensive Skin: Don't let the counter boy at Saks tell you what to do and definitely don't self-diagnose. Invest in dermatological professionals.

Manicures for Men: A true gentlemen is groomed, and that means a regular "mani-pedi." But no colored nails! The only men who should color their nails are those who perform under the name *Candelabra.*

he's very warm and friendly and proposes a "nightcap." Alice jokingly says, "You wanna go to a strip club?" Hugh is like, "Yeah! Let's go! Let's jump into a cab now!"

In the cab Hugh gets very friendly and goes, "Oh, aren't you the bitch from *People* magazine?" I'm like, "I'm only the person who had drinks with you three hours ago." He answers, "You look like Rod Stewart." But he did tell one funny story: He has different code names at hotels and he was really upset he had to drop his favorite one. For the longest time he would check into hotels under the name "Johnny Beaver," but his agent's assistant at CAA found it too offensive to call and ask for "Johnny Beaver" so he had to change it.

Don't ask me why, but I decide to save Hugh Grant's life that night. I tell him, "Hugh, we're not going to a strip club at three o'clock in the morning in Miami. You're just going to get yourself into trouble." In a drunken haze, we go to the dance club Billboard Live instead. He is still demonically possessed: His eyes dart around, he decides which chicks he's going to fix his eyes on, and then he beckons them. The bold chicks dangle their hotel room keys at him. Would you resist?

We move on to a joint called Rumi, where the Hugh Show continues. I finally extract myself from this sleazoid situation and head back to my hotel on my own to raid the mini-bar. I have a feeling Hugh had more to occupy himself with than twelve-dollar pistachio nuts when he got back to his hotel.

Steven Cojocaru

Mid-March:
Academy Awards, Shrine Auditorium

My Madonna moment. She's in a Goth-princess look with Rapunzel hair and a big skirt. Now, I was never the biggest Madonna fan, to be honest with you, but I have some respect for the way she pushes the envelope.

As she's coming down the red carpet, everybody is screaming "Madonna!" It's very loud, like a football match except everybody has tape recorders. One of the reasons I became successful on the red carpet is because my pipes are louder than anybody else's. I have giant vocal cords. I scream my questions at her. Most stars, when they can't hear you, say, "Pardon me? Excuse me, I can't hear you. Can you repeat the question?" Madonna wails, "WHAT?" She sounds like a Teamster.

I start to ask her about her fashion and she morphs into the Queen of England. She has that clipped British accent going. I say, "Tell me who you're wearing." She looks at me, rolls her eyes, and answers, "Ugh, I don't want to talk about fashion." I look at her with my snarky big mouth and go, "Well, then what do you want to talk about, brain surgery?" That's good. She seems to appreciate my moxie. So then she says, "My top is by Dolce & Gabbana and my skirt is by Olivier Theyskens. I'm an equal-opportunity dresser." Great quote. See, it wasn't that painful!

Madonna at the Oscars minutes before crushing me by not
wanting to gab about fashion. *(©Corbis)*

Early April:
Dinner for John Galliano, Brentwood

Joel Silver produced the *Die Hard* movies, *The Matrix*, and everything in between. I call him a mega-mega-mega-producer, and he invites little ol' me to a party that he and his wife, Karen, are having for **John Galliano**, the brilliant designer for Christian Dior. I'm in Joel Silver's amazing house to end all houses. He takes everybody on a tour and talks to us about the architecture, what he calls "Mexican modernism." The walls are glass. When he pushes a button, they disappear. The digs are so cool and high-tech, I nickname him the Jewish James Bond.

It's then I realize it's a tiny dinner party—John, Joel, Karen, **Salma Hayek**, and L.A. glamour girl Jen Mayer, Ralph Lauren's publicist. Joel pulls out all the stops. He's snagged the sushi chef from Ginza Sushi-Ko on Rodeo Drive—considered one of the greatest sushi chefs in the world. Dinner is ten courses. John Galliano is incredibly shy—he wanted to hear more about Hollywood because it was one of his first trips out West.

I'm feeling particularly welcome when Salma decides to put her foot in her mouth and disrespect me. Now, Salma is a smart woman. You sit and talk to Salma and she's got more there than most stars. I'm at this dinner as a private citizen—not a journalist. But Salma's worried.

Salma is telling us this story about going to a spa in Mexico with **Ashley Judd**, Salma's boyfriend, **Ed Norton Jr.**, and Ed's uncle. They were all naked in the sauna. Salma felt really nervous about being nude, she said, but she admired Ashley for not caring. Now Salma, who loves telling stories, turns to me and says, "I hope you're civilized enough that you're not going to write about this in *People* magazine." I found that very condescending. I took a sip of my wonderful wine and said, "Salma, you insult me. You're being ridiculous." I left it at that. Until now.

Late April: U.C.L.A., Nickelodeon Kids' Choice Awards

There's a rule that a celebrity should never walk more than three feet unassisted. So I do a lot of interviews from golf carts. I sat with **Sarah Jessica Parker**, fresh off the stage as host of the MTV Movie Awards, when she had her diamonds practically ripped off her neck by an on-the-clock Harry Winston security guard. She never missed a beat of our chitchat about hemlines and stilettos. Right now, I'm interviewing **Drew Barrymore** on a golf cart. She's at the Kids' Choice awards and Lord knows, she can't get to the auditorium by herself. She's very giddy, open, and sweet—that's because we've seen each other a million times. With stars, it helps to have context.

There's a rule that a celebrity should never walk more than three feet unassisted.

Like knowing that her backyard was a Hobbit warren of guest houses. This was the backyard to the love bungalow she

Things you might not have know about Drew Barrymore: She gives good interview while riding in a golf cart and she's a sucker for karaoke. *(©AFP/Corbis)*

lived in when she was married to **Tom Green**, which is now a burned-down love bungalow, so there are two sad things about that place. But nevertheless: The place was so self-contained. It was an amusement park. In one of the guest houses was a game room and full-on karaoke. I mean, a stage, huge sound system, microphone, and digital karaoke machine. There also was an air hockey table and pinball machines. At the top of the property was a tiki bar with a grass roof and Polynesian decor. They had their own world back there.

May: Interview, Chateau Marmont, L.A.

It's 9 A.M. and I'm up this early so that I can interview this no-name actress. This is my annual spring assignment, reporting for *People*'s "50 Most Beautiful People" issue. It's 1997 and the actress's name is **Catherine** something or other. I have to look it up: **Zeta-Jones**. What kind of name is that? The studio is pushing her hard. I think, "She's going to have one movie, *The Mask of Zorro,* and then she'll go away."

We've decided to meet at the Chateau Marmont, on the Sunset Strip. It's this castlelike hotel with a gorgeous exterior courtyard where celebrities like to get interviewed because it's intimate and people try hard to pretend not to notice that stars *are right over there!* **John Belushi** O.D.'d there. **Greta Garbo** used to live there. **Keanu** lived there.

When I walk in, I'm blown away. Her beauty is unnerving. Porcelain-white, creamy, beautiful skin. Greenish brown cat eyes. She has the most in-your-face beauty, like somebody slapped you across the face. Plus she's not made up at all, which is annoying. And she's goofy and has a great sense of humor. What I like most about her is that she's an eater. She isn't like these anorexic Hollywood stars who eat like birds. She has bacon and eggs and any woman who can eat me under the table has my immediate respect.

She's also somewhat gutsy, something I can't say about too many stars. She tells me she's had a tracheotomy and never talked about it before. She choked when she was a kid. Now she has a big scar, doesn't want to hide it, and she's so tired of all of these makeup artists who would constantly try to mask it. It's light, hardly noticeable, but it's there.

Fast-forward to now: Catherine and **Michael** swoop by me on the red carpet and don't stop to show me some love.

When you become famous, you change.

When you become famous, you change.

Summer Premiere Season:
L'Ermitage, Beverly Hills

The social politics of movie premieres is something everybody in Hollywood deals with constantly: You've just spent two hours of your life in a darkened theater, watching a terrible film. You felt like a tumor is developing while you're watching it. What do you say after? You don't gush, and Less Is More.

At the *Full Frontal* premiere party at the tony L'Ermitage Hotel in Beverly Hills, I run into **Julia Roberts**. She does the red carpet alone—her new hubby Danny Moder came later. Julia looks much, much better (and happier) than she did in the film, since director Steven Soderbergh had her in a cropped wig for the entire shoot. In the flick, she played an actress playing a journalist and I'm still not sure why she didn't call me for research. Maybe because she was playing a serious, bonafide journalist?

Now Julia is the type of devastating charmer who really gets along with guys. She's seen my clown act on *Today* and

In a Versace blazer, five-dollar vintage Levis, and bad hair at the American Fashion Awards, June 2001, New York City
(©*Jennifer Graylock*)

blows me away by offering a compliment about how she likes the Thursday segments with me and the gang. Flattery will get you everywhere, Julia. But then she bursts my bubble and decides to playfully bust me. "But did you have to copy one of my old hairstyles?"

She kicks up the charm factor, and she's now my chum (at least in my mind). She introduces me to Danny when he shows up. Their marriage is very fresh, maybe a month or two old, and they are in deep swoon. They are both very down to earth—he looks like an off-duty surfer. They let me into the their love-fest, and we have a verbal ménage-a-trois. I'm still waiting for them to call me so I can go to a sleepover at their house.

Of course, I don't tell her that I had issues with the film. So I decide to accentuate the positive: I say, "This movie really nails L.A." She answers very graciously, "I'm glad you got that." Sometimes I say, "You gave great eyebrow" or "Your highlights were really working overtime." Anything to make them feel that I was, at least, there. Julia and I have a Hallmark moment. We both leave feeling good. That's the way I like it.

September:
Emmys Post-Awards Dinner

It's mid-September, the hottest month in L.A., and the Emmys are brutal. I've been standing in my spot on the red carpet from one o'clock to five in a *velvet suit* in the blazing heat. At one point, with my hair gel dripping into my eyes, I think **Dennis Franz** is **Debra Messing** and I feel him up.

Last year's Emmys were particularly intense. They had been canceled twice because of 9/11. I didn't want to go, but my *People* superiors were adamant. I said, "How could you put me at risk? If I were al-Qaeda, I'd go straight for **Doris Roberts**. Hit us where it hurts." They said, "This is your community, and you need to be seen."

So I went. **Ellen DeGeneres** as host, was wonderful—soulful, smart, funny. Exactly what we needed. **Barbra Streisand** sang "You'll Never Walk Alone," and that got everybody. It was so moving. Afterward, at the Unity Dinner, my friend Heidi Schaffer the power publicist approached me. "Where's your table?" she asked. I said, "It's between Chechnya and Bosnia." She answered, "Well, honey: I'm giving you your Hanukkah present early."

She sat me at Barbra's table. By now you should know how much Barbra means to me. Word at the table was that Barbra was coming at a very specific time and needed a very specific chair and specific light.

At the table was Gary Smith, the producer of the Emmys, and his whole family—Auntie Mitzi, Uncle Moishe, all of them. We all knew our leader was coming. When she finally got to the table, they all turned to mush. Except me. At this point in my career, after years of interviewing celebrities, I believe in that line from **Patti LaBelle**: We all bleed and we all pee. Now, Barbra may have someone who urinates for her, I'm not sure.

Barbra appeared to be all nerves and tics and shaky, with her eyes lowered. We went around the table and introduced ourselves. When we got to me, I just gushed. "That was so gorgeous, Barbra. Amazing," She gave me the most condescending nod of her chin and a look on her face that said, "I know." After that, she had her head down and barely spoke. I think she broke down and talked to me when she asked for a bread stick. She had two and left.

There are certain things my mother doesn't want to know: Elizabeth Taylor has peach fuzz. And Barbra can be a brat.

November:
Tom Hanks and Rita Wilson's House,
Children's Action Network Benefit

I'm at **Tom Hanks** and **Rita Wilson**'s beach house in Malibu. It's a Cape Cod–style house, with a patio about two feet away from the ocean. My first trauma is that the house is so close to the water, the sea air is making my hair frizz. This is a few years back and I was still young and very self-involved. I've changed. Okay, not really.

Every year, a group of stars—**Goldie**, **Rita**, **Kate Capshaw**, **Sally Field**—hold a benefit at their house for the Children's Action Network, which helps kids in need. They get a fashion designer to do a runway show in their house (clearly, they have the space). It's a hot, big ticket. You get to see stars in their house, which is a window into their world. It's a privilege. So you do the dust test. You look in the medicine cabinet. You fix your peepers on everything.

I head to the deck, and out there is someone so beautiful you could only conjure her up in a fantasy: **Michelle Pfeiffer**, looking out at the ocean, lost in contemplation. Her eyes are almost translucent. So my job is to get quotes, to cover the party. I'll get in trouble if I don't. But she looks so peaceful and in her own space. Plus she's notoriously press-shy.

So I clear my throat and go up to her. "Excuse me, Ms. Pfeiffer, I'm here from *People* magazine, and we're covering the event today and I'd really like to talk to you." She gives me a guarded, "Yes." And something happens. We click. I

I wanted to be adopted by the Hanks. Who doesn't?
(©Reuters NewMedia Inc./CORBIS)

started with my dishy style and said something like, "There's a lot of women here and the gossip must be flying back and forth. What have you heard?" That breaks the ice.

This year it's **Giorgio Armani**'s turn to do the runway in Rita's house. He dressed the waiters—these topless, hunky waiters with enormous pectoral muscles and chiseled abs—in sarongs. So Michelle and I started to dish about the guys. And shy Michelle really opens up when it comes to sizing up a hunky waiter with a six-pack. We had a little girlish, giggly moment.

Steven Cojocaru

December:
Beverly Hills, Fire and Ice Ball

I'm sitting on stools with the *Friends* girls: **Jennifer, Courtney,** and **Lisa.** I have the exclusive to interview them right before the Fire and Ice Ball, which is this huge benefit to raise money for the U.C.L.A. Women's Cancer Research Fund that they're hosting. I can say they've come a long way.

When they were young girls, when *Friends* was just starting out, they put up this wall with journalists—maybe they were just afraid. The fame came so suddenly, and it took a while for them to adjust. But now, as grown women, they really know how to handle themselves. I am smitten with Jennifer—she's most clownish of them all. When you talk to Lisa and Courtney they are a little more reserved.

I give all of them credit—none of them looks "done." They have resisted a lot of plastic surgery. I say, "Not like this one star whose lips are so blown up she can't speak." And they go, "Who?" I say, "I'll tell you off camera." As soon as the cameras are off—the *second* the cameras go off—Lisa Kudrow goes, "Okay, who's the girl with the big lips?"

Cleavage anyone? The *Friends* girls may be polished pros now, but they still like to dish the dirt. (*©AFP/Corbis*)

—m—

THE OSCARS AND THE MONSOON-PROOF TRESSES

March 24, 2002

H ere's a page from my diary—minus the dry corsage I saved from prom night so long ago—highlighting my Oscars day.

8 A.M.

I'm down to the wire. I have two hours to make my Sophie's Choice: a black sequined blazer that **Donatella Versace** sent to me from Italy via her assistant Nunzio, or the sleek black satin jacket from Lord's, my favorite rock-and-roll-formalwear boutique. By noon, I need to be in a car, heading to the biggest day of my year, and I have to make a choice. This is going to rip my heart out. But the Oscars demand nothing less than the highest drama.

First comes grooming. I shower and douse my cracked face with La Prairie hydrating mist. Then La Prairie moisturizer. Then I put on eye pads to bring down the cruel puffiness around my eyes. The entire time, I'm still debating the blazer. I fret that it gives me a kind of Circus, Circus casino-floor-host look. Can I really wear this to the most coveted invite of the year, the *Vanity Fair* post-Oscars bash at Morton's? This is my first time going, with a real invitation to go inside—beyond the velvet rope. I can't look like I should be dealing chips to people at the two-dollar blackjack table.

9 A.M.

Thankfully, distraction comes first: makeup. I'll be doing the red carpet for *Access Hollywood,* and they've sent over a makeup person to do a little light foundation, highlighting stuff, and a lot of concealer (unfortunately, applied with a paint roller). I'm strenuously against having my eyebrows penciled in. I don't want to look like Joan Crawford.

Then comes the Director of My Hair, my beloved Byron. He looks like one of the members of Destiny's Child in white clogs, white jeans, and a gigantic gold ring on his finger that says MEOW. Byron spends an hour doing my hair. It takes about ten minutes to blow it out straight and then forty-five to use up an entire bottle of hair spray to keep it that way.

11 A.M.

Jenny, my stylist, was completely fed up with me. Jenny is in her early thirties, has caramel hair, and reminds me of a Jewish

J. Lo. I felt like she was my mom, dressing me for the prom.

Going overboard on my look as usual, I'd had this initial vision of a suit, burgundy or dark blue or emerald-green velvet (my mother would be so proud). But Jenny couldn't find it. I sent her to the four corners of the earth for that outfit—elegant with a little rock-and-roll touch—but nothing close. She pulled heaps of clothes and we set up a little lab in my old, starving writer's apartment—a frat boy's barren crash pad at this point. All potential outfits went on a clothing rack. For two weeks, I fretted and discarded. You couldn't find the phone or the furniture. There were just empty pizza boxes and clothing everywhere. All the outfits were on "loan" from Lord's boutique—you don't pay for anything as long as you dry-clean it when you're done and you return it in within a day or two. Rockers, like **Steven Tyler** and **Jon Bon Jovi**, shop there so I knew I was in good company.

The fact is, I needed *two* drop-dead ensembles: one for the red carpet, and one for the *Vanity Fair* party. I was leaning toward the black satin suit for my red carpet stint, and, to go gangbusters for *Vanity Fair,* a pair of white satin pants, a sheer Dolce & Gabbana white silk shirt, and sleek Gucci boots. I don't know what had gotten into me with the all-white getup—I guess it was the ghost of David Bowie's rock-chic style haunting me again. I had actually worn the pants to the Oscars three years ago, which is a bit of a fashion no-no, but you should know by now that I like breaking the rules.

Jenny kept pushing a burnt-gold satin tuxedo shirt for the Oscars suit. But it had ruffles. I said, "I look like Ricky Ricardo.

These will not do." Jenny shook her head and said, "They look fine." But the ruffles were splashing out everywhere. We had minutes to spare. "Do you want to tape them down?" Jenny said, in a flash of inspiration. So we tamed the ruffles.

I need to break open the secret of the male thong. I believe men should be held up to the same visible-panty-line standard as women. That's something a lot of men don't think about. But if you're building your wardrobe and you don't know where to start, you might begin by getting the male thong. There is something that International Male puts out and it's called The Sock. I'll leave the rest to your imagination. The only problem with The Sock is it's made out of very thin cotton and it's flimsy. It's supposed to give you support but it doesn't really. I was worried about The Sock letting me down and making me look like I was primed for a prostate examination. These are the kinds of ridiculous things you think about when you write "Fashionista" in the occupation box on your tax return. Maybe in my next life, I'll come back as a microbiologist who will never have to waste gray matter contemplating a male thong.

12 P.M.

My car is waiting outside to take me to the Kodak Theater, the new location for the Oscars. I take one last forlorn look at the Versace blazer.

12:02 P.M.

Another look.

12:06 P.M.

Donatella, don't hate me.

12:15 P.M.

Once I leave the house, it's done. I don't torture myself. The car ride to the Oscars is actually time for me to decompress from Byron, Jenny, and all the bustle. I don't like to move around in the car too much because if I do too much frantic activity, like leaning over to open a bottle of water, it might make the careful soufflé that is my hairstyle de-pouff and frizz. But the fretting is really unnecessary: Byron does such a thick coating of hair spray—I'm not going to say what products he uses, it's like KFC, it's eleven secret spices—that he signs an affidavit and guarantees me in blood that my hair won't frizz. It lasts for like eighteen hours.

1 P.M.

I get to the Kodak before all the stars do. Back when the Oscars were at the Shrine Auditorium in downtown L.A., you came out right onto the red carpet. This year, I got dropped off in the middle of Hollywood and Highland and I had to walk on the sidewalk past all the souvenir shops with **Marilyn Monroe** plates and **David Hasselhoff** beach towels.

I make my way across the red carpet. Most of the junior reporters are already there, standing and waiting with the name of their publication taped to the ground in front of them. I remember those days. It is so dehumanizing. You're all crammed together, Air India in-flight magazine up against *People* up against an Italian fashion newsletter. Print people get relegated to the middle and the tail end of the carpet. It's all about the television crews, who get the prime real estate right off the street. The beginning of the carpet is one of the best places to be because the stars are fresh. They just got out of their car. They are amiable and talkative. By the middle, their publicist does all the dirty work and lies for them, saying: "Oh she has to go, she's at the top of the show. I'm so sorry I have to pull her."

I find the *Access Hollywood* crew and they send me upstairs, to the balcony with Shaun Robinson. Pat O'Brien and Nancy O'Dell will be on the red carpet interviewing the stars. On the balcony, with E! and CNN, we have the perfect perch to catch the entire carpet drama. Our job will be to watch all the stars and react. Basically, I'm a paid heckler. I really love being on camera with Shaun because she treats me like the naughty boy that I am. Being up on the balcony brings out all the mischievous prankster demons in me—I have visions of taking water bombs and throwing them on different stars. Of course, all of this looks great on television. In real life, though, the view is a bit more mundane. You're mostly stuck looking at neon souvenir shop signs and Ripley's Believe It or Not Museum.

3:30 P.M.

Publicists have overtaken the red carpet. One of the little-known (or seen) parts of the Oscars is all the cell-phoning going on between stars in their limousines and the publicists who are telling them when to show up. Lots of stars get told to circle the block because they get there too early. And if you get there too early, you're considered a complete loser. You are F-list. The biggies come the last half hour, between four-thirty and five.

Then there are those who are always the last to arrive. Like **Cher.** I remember she was the last to arrive at the Oscars the year that *Titanic* was nominated. She wore that gigantic flying saucer on her head. I shouted to her, "Cher, Cher. Come here and talk to *People.*" But she was not coming near reporters. My childhood idol or not, finally I lost it and barked, "Cher, if you do not come and talk to me you're not allowed in. Will you get your butt over here and talk to me right now?" She seemed to like direction, so she came over and talked.

Here's the problem: Forget about food and forget about tinkling. You're in the sweltering heat, but you can't hydrate because there's nowhere to whiz. And you're starving because you're too nervous to eat in the morning and so you're kind of blacking out from not eating. Low blood sugar and a full tank. A bad combination.

4 P.M.:
THE PEEK OF THE CARPET

The first stars start to make their way into the Kodak. We're getting a live feed from the carpet and I'm playing bad cop to Shaun's good cop. I love it. Now is when the real product placement fashion parade heats up.

The way Oscar fashion works is that weeks before, when the nominations are announced, the courting and the bribery of stars begins. It's gotten completely out of control. Millions of dollars of publicity are now on the line and that's taken all the civility out of it. Each star's stylists are seduced by the designers at the couture houses—they get sent to the shows in Europe, and then the stylists "recommend" a gown or a necklace to their clients.

Now, most stars are just borrowing jewels or gowns for the night—and there's a security guard who will take it all back the gems the next morning. But if one stars starts wearing the same jewelry house show after show, your well-waxed eyebrow starts to arch. And bauble-advertising stars don't come cheap—the range of payments can go from several hundred thousand to seven figures. They will say that these glittering gems are just "tossed on," but I know different. Everybody is saying this is the future: product placement. Well, my underwear is sponsored by Victoria's Secret and my lip liner is by M.A.C.

4:25 P.M.

Did I tell you that I'm colossally bored? My bar is really high. Usually I get tipped off in advance about the outfits. Sunday morning, reps for the designers call me to say, "It's confirmed that so and so is wearing this." But it amazes and frustrates me how these stars—who have the world's greatest clothes from **Chanel**, **Yves Saint Laurent**, and **Balenciega** sent to them—still manage to screw it up.

Case in point: **Gwyneth**. She's wearing this outfit that will haunt her for a long time. It's a Goth **Alexander McQueen** gown that shows off her sagging boobs with black Elvira eyeliner and yodeling Heidi hair. It's all over the map. People still ask me, "What was she thinking?" And I think that people like Gwyneth and **Cameron Diaz** are such golden girls, such It Girls, that they feel like they can do no wrong. Gwyneth probably walks around to this day going, "Nobody got me. Nobody got the artistic statement I was making." For trying an edgy runway look, I give her credit.

4:40 P.M.

I take it all back. **Renée Zellweger** walks by in a stunning black satin Carolina Herrera ball gown. All I can say is "Wow." **Nicole Kidman** floats past in with her soft pink chiffon Chanel gown. This is what the Oscars are really all about.

5 P.M.

The entire time I was obsessing: When do I change into my *Vanity Fair* outfit? The ceremony started and I went straight home, got into my party clothes, and taped down my nipples. I had to. In the white satin shirt, I looked like I had on the high beams. **J. Lo** does exquisitely well with this look. But mine are not as luscious and compliant as hers. So I put clear Scotch tape across them.

Then I had to head to Burbank for my telestrator bit. I've become known for this segment because I draw silly things all over the footage: mustaches, tan lines, panty lines—I zero in on everything. Thankfully nobody is turning the tables on me, because I think The Sock wasn't quite in position. The next night, when Pat O'Brien came out of my segment to introduce the

Telestrator madness! *Access Hollywood*'s Nancy O'Dell and Pat O'Brien don't have the heart to tell me I'm no John Madden. But they've taught me more than I could have learned in Broadcasting for Beginners.
(Photo courtesy of Access Hollywood*)*

DEMONS OF THE RED CARPET

Antisocial stars who might think about closing escrow on that split-level cave in the Himalayan Mountains.

Calista Flockhart: No one looks more miserable or pained to be on the red carpet. Or bolts faster in her Jimmy Choos from reporters. Ally McBrat.

Helen Hunt: Testy, testy, testy. How can someone be so cranky and uptight while wearing a free Gucci gown? Silk charmeuse is enough to plaster a smile on my face for an entire day.

Madonna: Despite the advanced Kabbalah classes, not a giver on the red carpet. "So what if the hordes want to talk to me, let them eat macrobiotic cake . . ."

next thing, he said something about me "really filling up my pants." (I went and burned The Sock. I'm still searching for a better-insulated male thong.)

8 P.M.

The night has turned suddenly chilly, and now I'm freezing. There's nothing between me and the elements but a shirt with the consistency of one-ply Kleenex. I'm at the *InStyle* party at

DIVAS OF THE RED CARPET

Social butterflies who work it expertly.

Sarah Jessica Parker: No one bursts on to the red carpet with more gleeful sunny energy. And she gives good outfit too. Those self-help books were right: a good attitude is everything.

Halle Berry: Throw this approachable glamourpuss any question and she'll toss back a sassy fun answer. Plus, she could teach pigmies to slither sexily.

Meryl Streep: The greatest living actor is a coquette? I thought she'd hit me over the head with her Shakespearian Acting plaque when I gingerly approached the topic of fashion, but she dove right in with gusto. She was playful and engaging, probably the two most important red carpet traits.

Nicole Kidman: Plays it with just the right mixture of schoolgirl shyness and slap-you-in-the-face vampiness. Put her in a slit gown, and she'll give you carefully posed leg like no other.

Courtney Love: This uncensored wild child doesn't walk the red carpet, she explodes on it. It's never a dull moment with this loose cannon.

Debra Messing: She's happy to be on the red carpet and it shows on her beaming mug. The best manners of any red-carpet prowler. Mamma Messing did a good job.

DIVAS OF THE RED CARPET

Sandra Bullock: Miss Self-Deprecating herself. Got quip, will travel.

David Duchovny: A well-deserved honorary red carpet diva. Who says real men can't dish? A man who clearly can laugh at himself and fill out a size 42 long tux rather well.

Moomba, but honestly, I'm sort of cheating on *InStyle,* because all I'm thinking about is the *Vanity Fair* party.

Maybe this is because I had to labor so hard to get an invite. I really had to work the phones. I was in and then out and then in then out. They tortured me. They dump you by leaving you a voice message saying, "We can't accommodate you at the *Vanity Fair* party." They keep editing the list and "checking with **Graydon [Carter]**," the editor of the magazine. I heard this a lot in the days before. They would say his name in hushed tones, like he was some mythical figure. I offered to do cleanup. To be the men's room attendant. Anything. Why? Because it's the schmooze-a-thon of the year. It's pure high-octane glamour.

Finally they told me I had a window to come: 11 P.M.

11:30 P.M.

I'm waiting for **Ann Curry** in the parking lot of the Pavilions grocery store on Santa Monica Boulevard. She's going to go with me to the *Vanity Fair* shindig. You want to talk about reverse glamour? I'm frostbitten up to my collarbone. Where's that Versace blazer?

12:15 A.M.

Ann shows up in her car and we're whisked to Morton's, in West Hollywood. It's at Robertson and Melrose and it's limo gridlock. This gives me time to take in the giant klieg lights and this giant tree manicured in the shape of an Oscar. Outside the front door there are bleachers for the public and a velvet rope for the press types.

Soon enough we're in. And there is **Farrah Fawcett** looking kind of dazed and confused. **Diana Ross** sits in a booth with her huge mane of hair. It looks like steel wool stapled to her head. She looks like she's about to take a nap, to be perfectly honest.

Everywhere you turn there are stars. It's a big room that is just packed, packed, packed with stars. There's been a dangerous trend in L.A. where you get invited to a party, and then surprise: There's a V.I.P. room within the party for the stars and you're locked out. What I like about the *Vanity Fair* party is it's very democratic. People from all walks of life crammed into one room. It's fascinating to see people from the literary world and the art world and movie stars . . . that's what makes *Vanity Fair's* such a good party. The hype definitely pays off. When you're in there, there's electricity in the air.

But it's also clique on top of clique. **Mel Gibson** is in the back room with his cronies around him and smoking a cigar. He always finds the womb of the party and stays there. Gwyneth and Nicole have a little mutual-fan club going. People spill onto the dance floor and sprawl into banquettes. **Hugh Jackman** is so obviously the belle of the ball. It's interesting to see the aura around somebody who's really hot. He's wearing a very nice classic tux and he looks very dashing and dapper. I think: "*That's* what a leading man looks like."

There are some stars who have brain blackouts and misbehave. If you're going to do drugs, do it privately. Don't start smoking pot behind the plants, as the daughter of one music legend did. Or what about the famously buxom TV star and the British starlet who were snorting half of Peru in the women's bathroom?

The power keeps going out. I keep drinking vodka tonics. Soon enough Ann and I split up and I'm on my own. At 2:45 A.M. I get invited to the after-after party. But I have to be on air at 5 A.M. to do a morning dispatch for the *Today Show.* I need a break. I don't think my La Prairie can do it without some downtime. So I go home and hose off my dried, caked-on makeup.

4 A.M.

I give Byron a wake-up call so that he can redo my hair. He hates me and loves me simultaneously. He calls me Miss Crawford and I'm not amused. I get to Burbank and meet up with Ann Curry, who looks ridiculously fresh-faced despite the fact that I was with her hours ago and I know she hasn't slept. In minutes, we're on air. It's amazing how quickly you wake up when you have the opportunity to deconstruct Gwyneth's Heidi hair on national television.

NINE

MEET MY AGENT, JERRY SEINFELD

October, 2001: Private Room, 11 Madison Park Restaurant

I begrudingly entered The Establishment. I didn't full-out join, but I certainly dipped my pedicured toe in. Nora McAniff, who was then the president of *People* magazine, offered me a temporary membership. She hosted a dinner party for **Jeff Zucker**, the president of NBC Entertainment. As the former executive producer of the *Today Show*, Jeff was one of the biggies who'd shaped my career, and he'd just been kicked upward—way upward. The party would be the inner sanctum for heavy-hitters, held in a private room at 11 Madison Park, this fancy restaurant in midtown. I was very, very nervous.

Not because I didn't know which fork to pick up. Not because this was my first time seeing Matt Lauer socially. But because I didn't know what to wear. I didn't want to be a freak show. At the same time, I didn't want to compromise myself. This is an issue I see a lot—the dress-code confusion around

America's first TV family visiting with Cousin It. *(Photo courtesy NBC/*The Today Show*)*

the "professional party." A lot of my girlfriends call me in a tizzy. These are girls who work for major studios, who are powerful, and they call me completely undone: "I'm going to this party tonight and what should I wear?" they ask in a panic. I answer, "Fashion should not be torture." At this point in my life, that's my only rule. It should not be hard work. If you're that tortured, then bathe and wear all black. You can never go wrong emitting a pleasant scent while in the safe cocoon of a black ensemble.

But I have to admit: That night I was tortured. There's such a huge difference between dress codes in New York and Los Angeles. In L.A., I could get away walking into any high-class dinner looking like a rock star. The culture is a lot more forgiving. People say, "Oh, he's that crazy fashion guy. He can wear anything." It's so casual. In New York, it's so formal. "Rock star" is not amusing—it's tacky. Unless you're Lenny Kravitz.

I wanted to respect some shred of the dress code, but at the same time I wanted to be me. I knew what was appropriate would be wearing a nice suit. So I borrowed a Gucci suit, but when I put it on I looked like a pallbearer. Matt Lauer looks good in suits. I don't. I compromised and I did my version of formal conservative: skin-tight black leather pants by Roberto Cavalli with distressed leather so they were all rubbed out. It looked like the number five MTA bus drove over me and then decided to back up a couple of times. People must have thought, "Oh my God, he was in an accident." On top, I wore an orange-tangerine pink crinkled silk shirt with an embroidered snake on it. It was very flashy-wild and I wore it completely unbuttoned. One of the old-fashioned rules that still applies is: always accentuate your best feature. As far as I'm concerned my only good feature is my concave chest. I have half a pectoral and not a lot of chest hair (I'm still waiting for puberty to hit). At the right angle with the shirt open, I have that scrawny rock and roll chest that I like to show off when I can.

"Fashion should not be torture." At this point in my life, that's my only rule.

Dinner, in the form of passed hors d'oeuvres and chitchat, was served standing up. **Jerry Seinfeld** was in one corner. **Al Roker** was in another. Then, Nora approached me with news. Jeff Zucker had gone up to her and said, "You're not going to believe this, but of everybody in this room **Jerry Seinfeld** only wants to meet one person. He wants to meet Steven."

My mother is enthralled with two celebrities: **Matt Lauer** and **Jerry Seinfeld**. To her, they're the epitome of well-groomed, All-American, nice guys—and they have solid bank accounts. Pretty much perfection in her book. She wants me to be them more than anything. She's henpecked me for years about them. "Why can't you be more like Matt? Look at how polished Matt is. God put you beside Matt for a reason," she says. When she finally puts Matt on hold, she moves on to Jerry. "You should cut your hair like Jerry's. And wear nice sweaters like Jerry. That's the way to dress." If my mother was in a room with either of them, she'd probably knock back a Shirley Temple and then jump them.

No pole vaulting necessary. Nora takes me over to Jerry. He was kind and flattering. He said he enjoyed my work on the *Today Show.* He had no idea what his seal of approval meant. But I did. Nora and I were in the middle of renegotiating my contract, and it was at the boiling point that day. We had both agreed that we'd leave it alone for the duration of the dinner party. Now here was Jerry saying this, and he didn't realize how much he was selling me. When Jerry said, "You're doing a good job," I turned to Nora and smiled that "Jerry thinks I'm worth *x* dollars" smile. So nice Jerry Seinfeld got me a raise and my American Express card will always be grateful to him.

But then I made the mistake of telling Jerry that my mother was in love with him. "My mother wants me to be you," I told him. "There's electric shock treatments that she wants me to endure to become more Jerry-esque." He said to me, "Where does she live?" It turned out he was performing in Montreal soon and he offered a pair of tickets for my parents to see him, along with backstage passes. You can't imagine the delirium in my household when I called my mom to break this news. But then of course, she had issues. "We want to go, but we can't leave your sister behind—she would be devastated," my mom told me. "And then of course there's Auntie Rhoda and Uncle Rubin. You can't even mention Jerry Seinfeld without them bursting into tears. We'll have to get the smelling salts. Do you think you can get us five tickets?" I couldn't believe it—my mom was trying to be a vulture off Jerry Seinfeld's generosity. I said, "Mom—that is so nervy."

I had to bite the bullet and humiliate myself by calling Jessica Seinfeld to ask Jerry if we could have five tickets. It felt so wrong. I was so embarrassed. But Jessica and Jerry were so above and beyond lovely about it. I think Jerry understands what neurotic Jewish parents are and like the politics and the wild excitement that comes over respectable people when it comes to meeting a superstar. I sent him a Louis Vuitton tie to sheepishly say thank you, and he wore it at the performance.

So my parents and my sister and Auntie Rhoda and Uncle Rubin ended up backstage and met Jerry. It was the highlight of their lives. They must have driven him crazy—they probably never left the Green Room. They still talk about it to this day. I just saw Jessica Seinfeld at a lunch recently, and now *I'm* driving *her* crazy because every time I see her I bring it up: "Thank God most of mom's friends were wintering in Florida. Otherwise, she might have asked if they could bring along the Romanian Tabernacle Choir."

If I could plop a king-sized bed wrapped in Pratesi sheets in a makeup room, I'd turn that welcoming nook into my permanent sleeping quarters. I nearly do every Thursday when I'm on

THINGS YOU SHOULD NEVER SAY TO A CELEB

"Call me sentimental, but I remember when your wife was a call girl in the early 1990s."

"I heard you are hung like a . . . hamster."

"The next time my airbags deploy, I'll think fondly of your breasts."

"I was just telling your wife how buff your boyfriend is."

the *Today* show. I get to the studio bright and early on those mornings. Night owl that I am, I'm definitely in need of a "clear the makeup room" emergency session. In the makeup room, Katie will pop in and say hello and Matt will pop in, invariably, to run me down and affectionately make fun of how my foundation is applied with a blowtorch. He watches in stunned amazement as I dab on my Chanel cheek brightener. Matt, I'm perfectly willing to share. (During the commercial breaks, Matt, Katie, Ann, Al, and I catch up. We giggle, we dish. I'll tell them who's sleeping with whom in Hollywood. They were shocked when I told them about a very famous young pop singer with a propensity for showing off her belly button and which movie star she was said to be sleeping with. After grilling Donald Rumsfeld in the first part of the show, I think court-jester me is a relief to Katie and Co.

SHAMELESS KISS-UP THINGS YOU SHOULD SAY TO A CELEB (REMEMBER, ALWAYS APPEAL TO VANITY)

"You have Mona Lisa's smile and Britney Spears's butt."

"You haven't aged a day since Woodstock."

"You make Reese Witherspoon look like an octogenarian."

Every now and then, a window of opportunity will open and I'll get invited into a dressing room. Katie's dressing room is a power dressing room. It's not like a star's—it's like a working journalist's dressing room. There are much more paper and files in there than there are nail polish and makeup. Katie is one of the most open, unguarded people I've ever met. A lot of mega-famous people can be so closed and defensive. I call them alien life forms in Prada. Katie, though, is a bona fide human being. She's interested in you and asks questions about your life. I kind of have a little prepubescent crush on her. It's like when you're dazzled by a girl in class and you want to stick gum in her hair to get her attention.

Ann Curry, the news anchor for the show and my escort into the *Vanity Fair* Oscar party, is my conscience. She's so bright and passionate—she really wants to make a difference. Ann Curry and I recently had a poignant lunch at Michael's—it's the media publishing power restaurant. There's a whole pecking order where you sit and we sat at a very A-list table. **Tom**

Brokaw and **Tina Brown** were at the table next to us. It made me think that there's never a single moment where you feel "I've arrived." There's a lot of little moments. You think you're Cinderella, you come back to your real life, and your dog has defecated all over the house. You take off your glamour-boy hat and you morph back into a scullery maid, scrubbing the floors.

• • •

I know someone as over-the-top as me is ripe for parodying. I'm a walking cartoon character, but I never dreamed that Jimmy Fallon noticed. One Saturday evening in December, I was out to dinner with my friend Abby, kicking back margaritas, when my cellphone rang mid-burrito. It was my friend Sandi Shurgin, who lives on the East Coast. She told me that I had just been parodied on that night's *Saturday Night Live*.

I flew home. This was a very emotional moment for me. It was like the Beatles were about to be on Ed Sullivan, and I was Ringo, Paul, John, and George rolled in one. My first reaction was: I hope it was somebody good-looking from the show. I thought, Wouldn't it be awesome if it was **Jimmy Fallon**? I could deal with that. But then the neurotic thought came to me: What if it's a horrible impersonation? Who knows what they've done to me! I went through the scenarios—did they make fun of my hair? My teeth? Then my agent Kenny called me and said, "It's Jimmy Fallon."

I breathed this gigantic sigh of relief. The vain part of me was really happy. So I had a Zen moment. I turned off the phone and just waited for the show to begin. The waiting was so surreal—to sit in front of a television screen, passing the time to see someone play you on television.

Then the skit started. Its premise was that Donatella Versace, played by **Maya Rudolph,** had her own talk show, which was set in her marble bathroom in her palazzo. Her first guest was supposed to be Jean Paul Gaultier, but he got an earring infection and couldn't be on. "So I got stuck with this cheap fill-in," Donatella said from the bathtub. Then Jimmy came on in a brown wig—these were the last days of my life as a brunette—a pink feather coat, and hipster jeans. My wind-tunnel closed down. I was in shock.

Clearly, he had been watching VH1. The week before, I had done a guest appearance in a borrowed pinky-orange,

Jimmy Fallon nailed me on *Saturday Night Live* (except for the coif—he should have used my okra hair conditioner!) *(Photo courtesy of Broadway Video Enterprises)*

Mongolian lamb, ghetto-wild coat and custom-made, lace-up Henry Duarte jeans. But this was a cheap version of me. If you're going to do me, do me right. Don't get the $40 version of my Mongolian coat or the Guess version of my Duarte jeans. But Jimmy nailed the rest of the package. He was giggling and trying to get my smile. In the skit, Donatella says to him, "Steven, you look hideous—what have you done?" And Jimmy starts going off on plastic surgery jokes, but Donatella won't have any of it. "Get out!" she says. "You look hideous!"

As cheap an imitation as that was, they went overboard with Karl Lagerfeld, Donatella's next guest. It was **Mick Jagger**. I almost dropped dead thinking that Mick Jagger might actually know who I am. That my name might have actually hit his eardrum. This is the Living End, I thought. Here was Donatella, my first big celebrity brush, Mick Jagger, one of my greatest idols, and a two-bit version of myself.

The next morning, I sent Jimmy Fallon a black silk Versace thong. I wrote him a note: "Dear Jimmy: I laughed so hard, one of my veneers popped off." Then, at the MTV video awards last summer, I went to the after-party that Dreamworks threw for Jimmy because he had hosted the show. I walked in and he saw me immediately. I started wagging my finger at him, like "you're in trouble." His eyes brightened and he gave me the biggest bear hug. He was so sweet and warm. He said, "You're the only person that I've ever parodied that has sent me a gift and that meant a lot." But I said to him, "Next time, if there is a next time, you'd better get the hair right."

• • •

The thing is, even when I get my own hair right, people think I'm Steven Tyler. They either tell me I'm a dead ringer for him, or that I'm obsessed with him. It's ironic, because even though I've shamelessly ripped off his hairstyles, he's not one of my idols per se. Sure, I think he's incredibly cool and talented, but it's not like the worship I felt for the Cher-Mick-Prince troika of my teens and twenties.

It took meeting a Tyler offspring to make me want to be adopted by the rocker. I met Liv Tyler on an airplane—as you can see, I do some of my best work in airplanes. We first saw each other in the Admirals Club at JFK. She kept staring at me and I kept staring at her until I had to approach her. "Do you think there's any way we are related?" I asked her. She said,

TIPS ON HOW TO BE A STAR MAGNET ON THE RED CARPET

- Dab some embalming fluid behind your ears. The scent will be familiar to Cher.

- Make some part of your person a conversation piece. A gigantic hairdo carefully shaped to look like a bonsai tree is a guaranteed icebreaker.

- Offer breath mints—stars would walk barefoot on glass to get anything for free.

"I was thinking the exact same thing." Turns out Liv is one of the earthiest, most genuine and grounded celebrities I've ever met.

We got on the plane and started dishing celebrities big time. She's a big disher. I had some tabloids with me. When she went to take a nap, I looked at her sleep and she seemed so angelic. Then I saw an article in the tabloids about how much weight she had gained, and I wanted to flush it down the toilet. At least I hid it from her.

Toward the end of the flight, I asked if she would deliver a note to her father for me. She promised she would hand-deliver it. I ripped the Stylewatch page out of *People* magazine, circled my face, and wrote:

Dear Mr. Tyler (Papa?)

By any chance have you ever slept with a 5 foot tall Jewish woman in Montreal? People say we look alike. This is wildly flattering to me and probably devastating to you. Your daughter Liv is an extraordinary person—you must be very proud.

Sincerely, Steven

Flash-forward to the red carpet of the Golden Globes 2002. I look up and there's my twin brother right in front of me. I had never seen the likeness up close. It was startling. He radiated warmth and said, "I got your note. It was great." I answered, "Well, I apologize a thousand times if anybody says we look alike. You're the Rolls Royce and I'm the Hyundai." Then he said, "You, me, and Liv, we should have dinner." I called him a few times, but I haven't heard back yet. Steven, let's go get some dim sum and talk about our hair.

• • •

I was such the quintessential fan that even **Dana Carvey** spitting on me was beautiful. At the MTV Video Awards when he was the host, I was lucky enough to get in the front row in the mosh pit. Dana was so manic and hyper that he when he was doing his monologue, he spat on me. And I cried. It was a spiritual experience.

But I've changed since then. If I was a sycophant to the stars, now I'm jaded. I caught on early that the stars were a mess just like me. There will always be a part of me that's still a little dazzled by Hollywood.

I never really had a plan; I just knew I wanted to be on the red carpet. Where else but on a covered sidewalk in Hollywood could a kink in the armor like me shine? And to be perfectly shallow, where else could a homely wallflower transform into something at least visually passable? If we're doing that Neanderthal thing and grading my appearance on a scale of one to ten, I came to Hollywood and I was dancing around being a one. Through the Herculean efforts of my yoga trainer, pilates trainer, weight trainer, two hairdressers on the West Coast, three hairdressers on the East Coast, my eyebrow sculptor Anastasia, a wardrobe stylist, an herbalist, a raw food nutritionist, West and East Coast facialists, my dermatological guru Dr. Grossman, and my dentist-to-the-stars Dr. Glassman, I've made a leap from a one to maybe a passable five on a good day, and I'm at peace with that.

I endured all that only to come to the not-particularly-profound conclusion that when you fixate on your appearance, you paralyze personal growth. It's taken me borrowing against my 401K to pay the Pilates piper only to ultimately embrace perhaps the most simplistic of clichés: Beauty—and celebrity—is only skin deep. It sure takes a while for common sense to seep through these highlights.

And now for the wild sex and flashy clothes part: If the literary muse of my college years, Inga, got her own twisted soap-opera happy ending, why can't I?

Steven had no idea when he got up and sang at J. Lo's birthday party what he would be starting. He thought that J. Lo, his best friend in the entire world, would appreciate his singing an old Stones classic like "Satisfaction." So he rang a bell and Byron jumped out of the vintage Hermés bag he was stuffed into. He quickly touched up Steven's silky, perfectly-conditioned hair with his battery-operated flat iron. Steven got up and adjusted the haute couture Dolce tee he was wearing—the one that perfectly showed off his naturally rock-hard abs. He hit the stage and started softly singing. Then, as the crowd roared and applauded—J. Lo, Brad, Julia, Cameron, and Lenny were weeping—his voice lifted higher and higher. It was the most exquisite sound. It was Pavarotti in size-thirty-waist Cavalli snakeskin pants.

Tommy Mottola of Sony Records raced up to him afterward and offered him a $50 million recording contract and use of the Sony corporate jet for life. "You're not a fashion editor," he said, trembling. "You're a rock star." Steven recorded a CD that Spin called "an artis-

tic masterpiece up there with Revolver and Sticky Fingers." He toured the world and sang his heart out every night to thousands of adoring fans who all wanted to sleep with him. Then he took the $50 million—minus a small amount for personal expenses—and donated it to a foundation that bankrolled the projects of creative misfits. He moved to Paris and became a respected poet. He let his hair air-dry and never had to flat iron his naturally tousled mane again.